BBC

DOCTOR WHO

THE TWELFTH DOCTOR

GHOST STORIES

"Great superhero action."
GEEK GIRL PROJECT

"Does anyone ever really know what to expect from a Time Lord? Rhetorical question. Of course not. If you're a *Doctor Who* fan, it's a must-buy."
GRAPHIC POLICY

"Crisp, clean, and nicely animated action. 4 out of 5!"
NERDLY

"The color art by Dijjo Lima proves fantastic, well-suiting the bright, four-color aesthetic of the story."
KABOOOOOM!

"Welcome back, Doctor!"
CHUCK'S COMIC OF THE DAY

"Extremely well-balanced and paced extremely well."
CAPELESS CRUSADER

"Ivan Rodriguez displays an aptitude for bringing superhero-based artistry to life."
THAT'S NOT CURRENT

"Interesting character development, sharp dialogue, colorful and impressive artwork!"
BLOGTOR WHO

"The characterization is consistent with what was shown on TV [...] the art is gorgeous and detailed."
GAMING TREND

"Reminiscent of Pixar's *The Incredibles*!"
GEEK.COM

TITAN COMICS

SENIOR COMICS EDITOR
Andrew James

COLLECTION EDITOR
Lauren Bowes

ASSISTANT EDITORS
Jessica Burton & Amoona Saohin

TITAN EDITORIAL
Lauren McPhee

COLLECTION DESIGNER
Andrew Leung

PRODUCTION ASSISTANT
Natalie Bolger

PRODUCTION SUPERVISOR
Maria Pearson

PRODUCTION CONTROLLER
Peter James

SENIOR PRODUCTION CONTROLLER
Jackie Flook

ART DIRECTOR
Oz Browne

SENIOR SALES MANAGER
Steve Tothill

PRESS OFFICER
Will O'Mullane

COMICS BRAND MANAGER
Chris Thompson

ADS & MARKETING ASSISTANT
Tom Miller

DIRECT SALES & MARKETING MANAGER
Ricky Claydon

COMMERCIAL MANAGER
Michelle Fairlamb

HEAD OF RIGHTS
Jenny Boyce

PUBLISHING MANAGER
Darryl Tothill

PUBLISHING DIRECTOR
Chris Teather

OPERATIONS DIRECTOR
Leigh Baulch

EXECUTIVE DIRECTOR
Vivian Cheung

PUBLISHER
Nick Landau

Special thanks to Steven Moffat, Brian Minchin, Mandy Thwaites, Matt Nicholls, James Dudley, Edward Russell, Derek Ritchie, Scott Handcock, Kirsty Mullan, Kate Bush, Julia Nocciolino and Ed Casey for their invaluable assistance.

BBC WORLDWIDE

DIRECTOR OF EDITORIAL GOVERNANCE
Nicholas Brett

DIRECTOR OF CONSUMER PRODUCTS AND PUBLISHING
Andrew Moultrie

HEAD OF UK PUBLISHING
Chris Kerwin

PUBLISHER
Mandy Thwaites

PUBLISHING CO-ORDINATOR
Eva Abramik

For rights information
contact Jenny Boyce
jenny.boyce@titanemail.com

DOCTOR WHO: GHOST STORIES
HB ISBN: 9781785861697
SB ISBN: 9781785861703
Published by Titan Comics, a division of Titan Publishing Group, Ltd.
144 Southwark Street,
London, SE1 0UP.

A CIP catalogue record for this title is available from the British Library.
First edition: October 2017.

10 9 8 7 6 5 4 3 2 1

Printed in China.

Titan Comics does not read or accept unsolicited DOCTOR WHO submissions of ideas, stories or artwork.

www.titan-comics.com

DOCTOR WHO
THE TWELFTH DOCTOR

GHOST STORIES

WRITER: GEORGE MANN

**ARTISTS: IVAN RODRIGUEZ,
PASQUALE QUALANO & DENNIS CALERO**

COLORIST: DIJJO LIMA

**LETTERS: RICHARD STARKINGS AND
COMICRAFT'S JIMMY BETANCOURT**

BBC

DOCTOR WHO

THE TWELFTH DOCTOR

THE DOCTOR

A rogue Time Lord of Gallifrey. Never cruel or cowardly, he champions the oppressed across time and space. Adventure and travel are what he lives for – and danger always has a way of finding him!

GRANT

Thanks to the alien gemstone he absorbed into his body as a child, Grant can fly, is invulnerable and super-strong, and doesn't feel silly dressed up in a tight leather costume to fight crime in New York City.

LUCY

A top journalist and investigator, Lucy has a keen head for secrets and a sharp line in incisive prose. Mother of Jennifer, and now married to Grant, thanks to their adventure with the Doctor eight years ago.

PREVIOUSLY...

Together, the Doctor, Lucy, and Grant defeated the nefarious forces of Harmony Shoal. The world saved, and his love for Lucy reciprocated, Grant put away the costume, and the Doctor left Grant and Lucy to their new life together.

But the Doctor is terrible for picking at loose ends...

When you've finished reading this collection, please email your thoughts to doctorwhocomic@titanemail.com

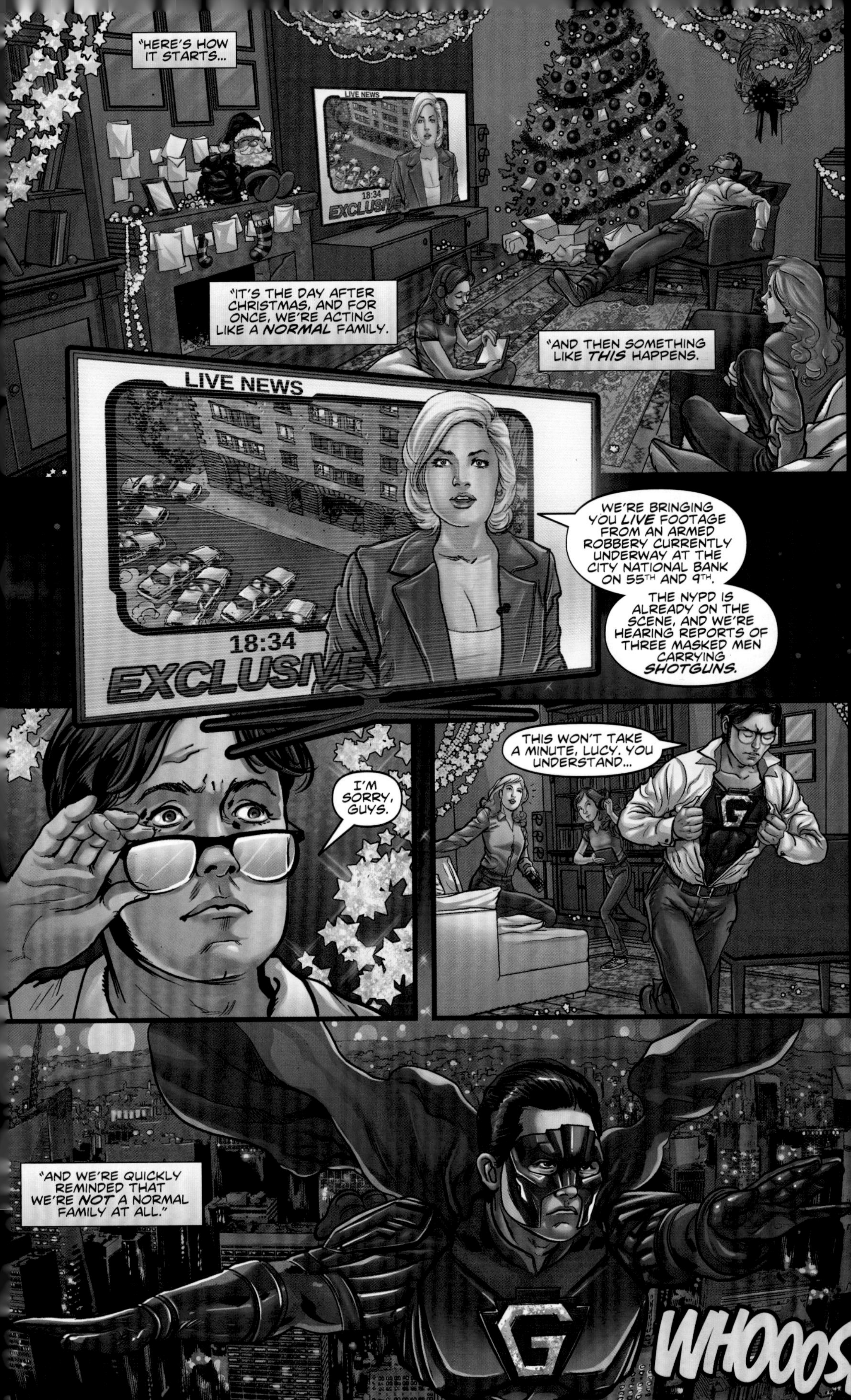
"HERE'S HOW IT STARTS...
LIVE NEWS
18:34
EXCLUSIVE
"IT'S THE DAY AFTER CHRISTMAS, AND FOR ONCE, WE'RE ACTING LIKE A NORMAL FAMILY.
"AND THEN SOMETHING LIKE THIS HAPPENS.
LIVE NEWS
18:34
EXCLUSIVE
WE'RE BRINGING YOU LIVE FOOTAGE FROM AN ARMED ROBBERY CURRENTLY UNDERWAY AT THE CITY NATIONAL BANK ON 55TH AND 9TH.
THE NYPD IS ALREADY ON THE SCENE, AND WE'RE HEARING REPORTS OF THREE MASKED MEN CARRYING SHOTGUNS.
I'M SORRY, GUYS.
THIS WON'T TAKE A MINUTE, LUCY. YOU UNDERSTAND...
"AND WE'RE QUICKLY REMINDED THAT WE'RE NOT A NORMAL FAMILY AT ALL."
WHOOOS

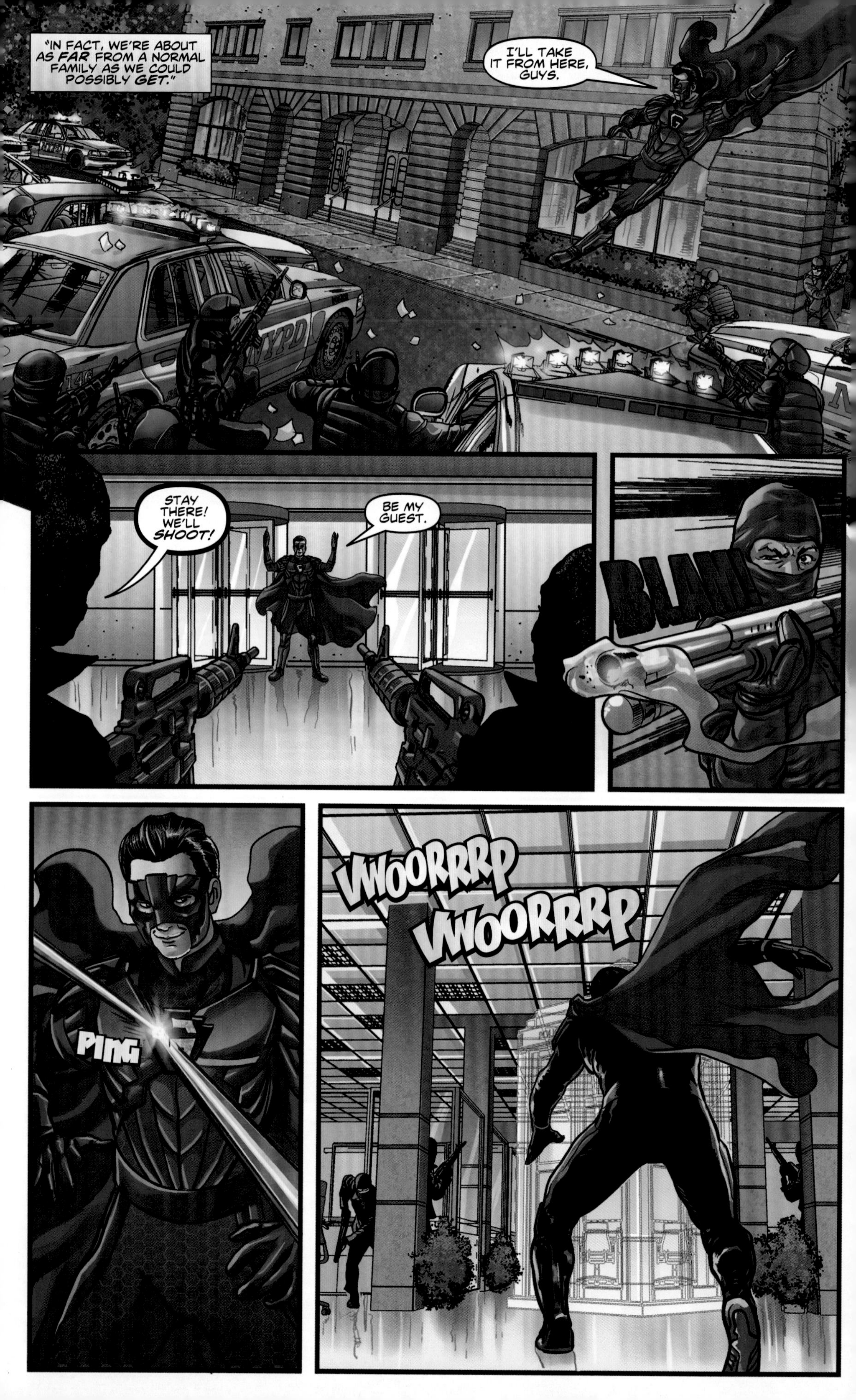
"IN FACT, WE'RE ABOUT AS FAR FROM A NORMAL FAMILY AS WE COULD POSSIBLY GET."
I'LL TAKE IT FROM HERE, GUYS.
NYPD
STAY THERE! WE'LL SHOOT!
BE MY GUEST.
PING
VWOORRRP
VWOORRRP

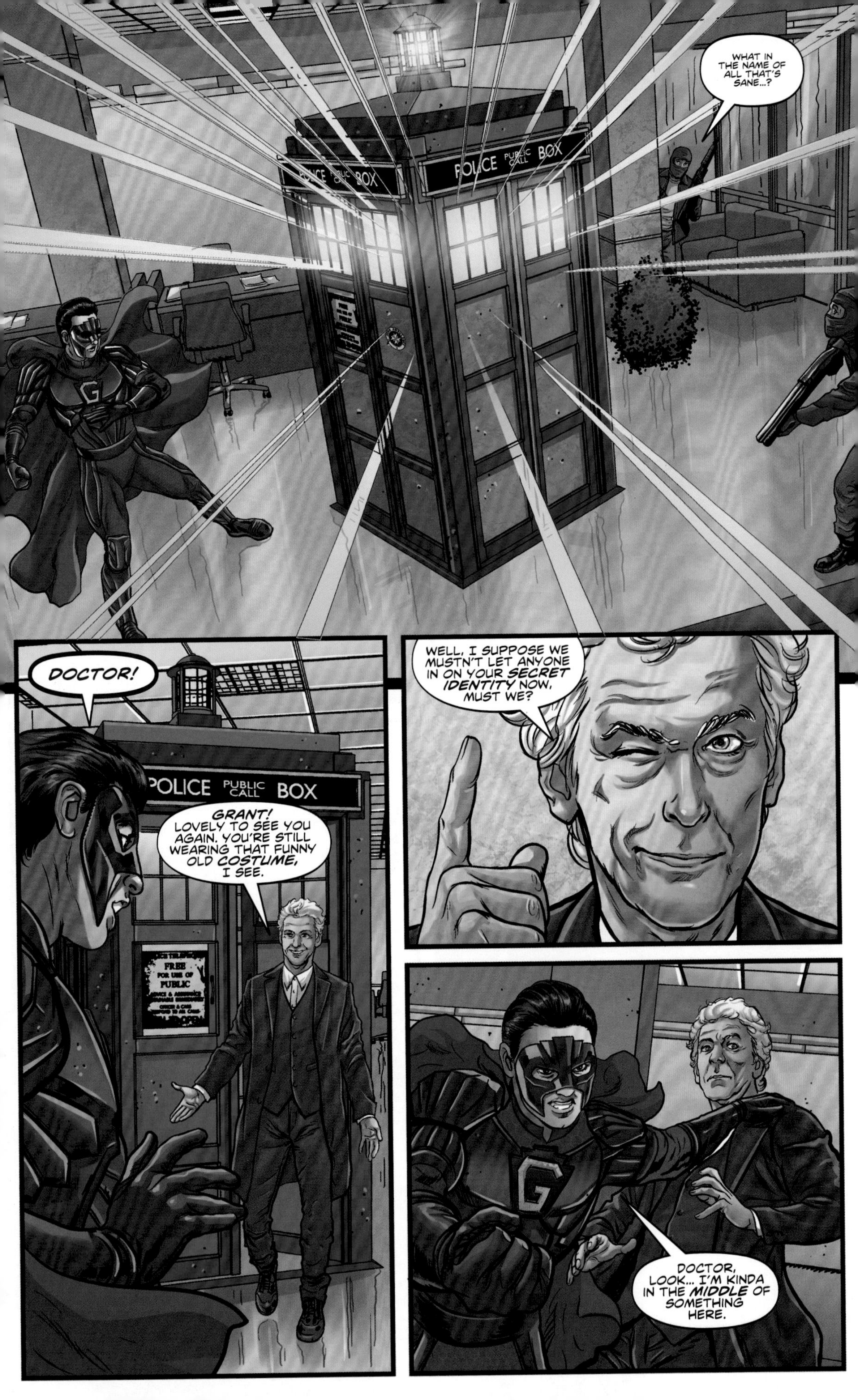
WHAT IN THE NAME OF ALL THAT'S SANE...?
POLICE PUBLIC CALL BOX
DOCTOR!
POLICE PUBLIC CALL BOX
GRANT! LOVELY TO SEE YOU AGAIN. YOU'RE STILL WEARING THAT FUNNY OLD COSTUME, I SEE.
WELL, I SUPPOSE WE MUSTN'T LET ANYONE IN ON YOUR SECRET IDENTITY NOW, MUST WE?
DOCTOR, LOOK... I'M KINDA IN THE MIDDLE OF SOMETHING HERE.

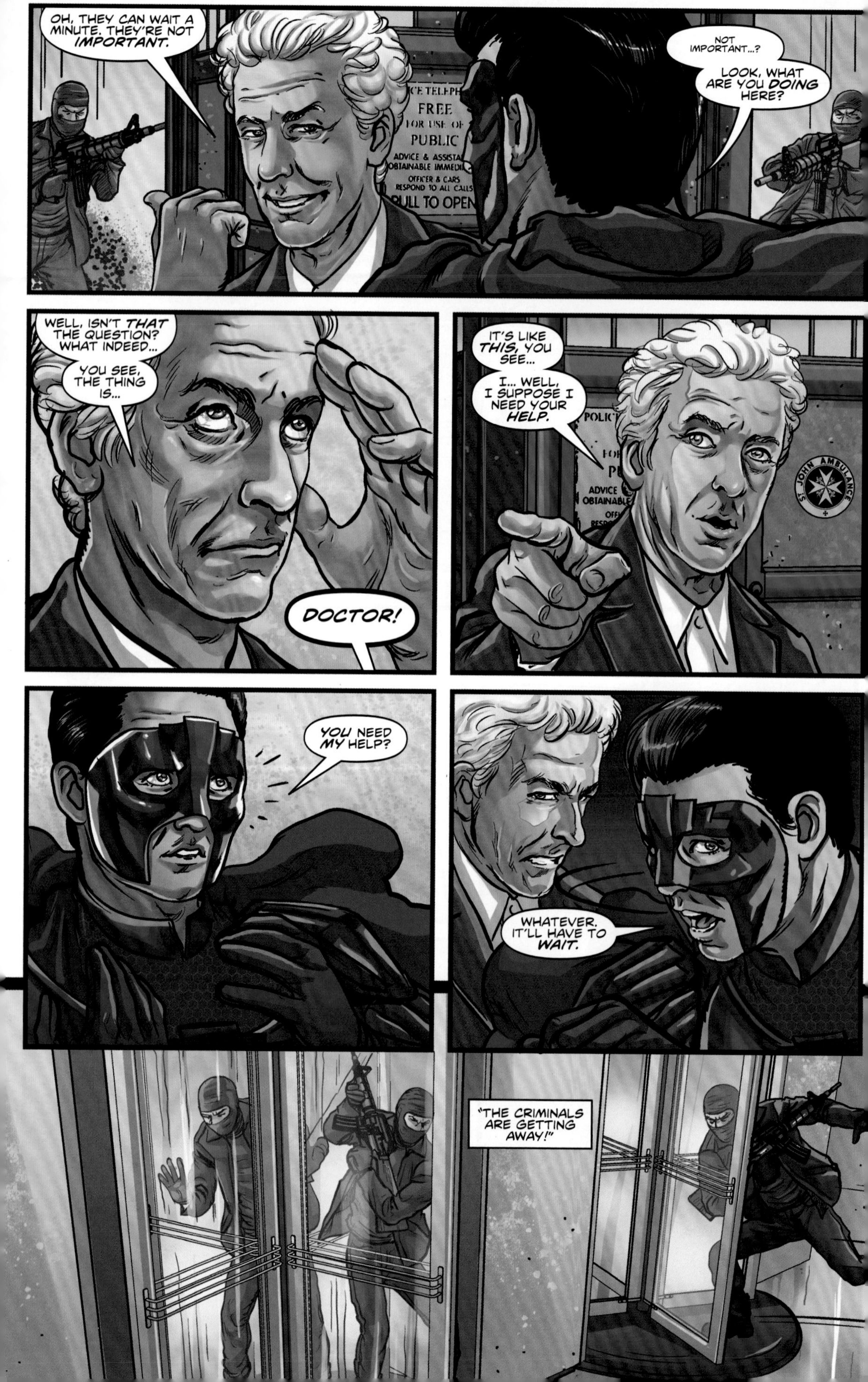
OH, THEY CAN WAIT A MINUTE. THEY'RE NOT *IMPORTANT*.
NOT IMPORTANT...?
LOOK, WHAT ARE YOU *DOING* HERE?
FREE
FOR USE OF
PUBLIC
ADVICE & ASSISTA
OBTAINABLE IMMEDI
OFFICER & CARS
RESPOND TO ALL CALLS
PULL TO OPEN
WELL, ISN'T *THAT* THE QUESTION? WHAT INDEED...
YOU SEE, THE THING IS...
DOCTOR!
IT'S LIKE *THIS*, YOU SEE...
I... WELL, I SUPPOSE I NEED YOUR *HELP*.
ST. JOHN AMBULANCE
YOU NEED *MY* HELP?
WHATEVER. IT'LL HAVE TO *WAIT*.
"THE CRIMINALS ARE GETTING AWAY!"

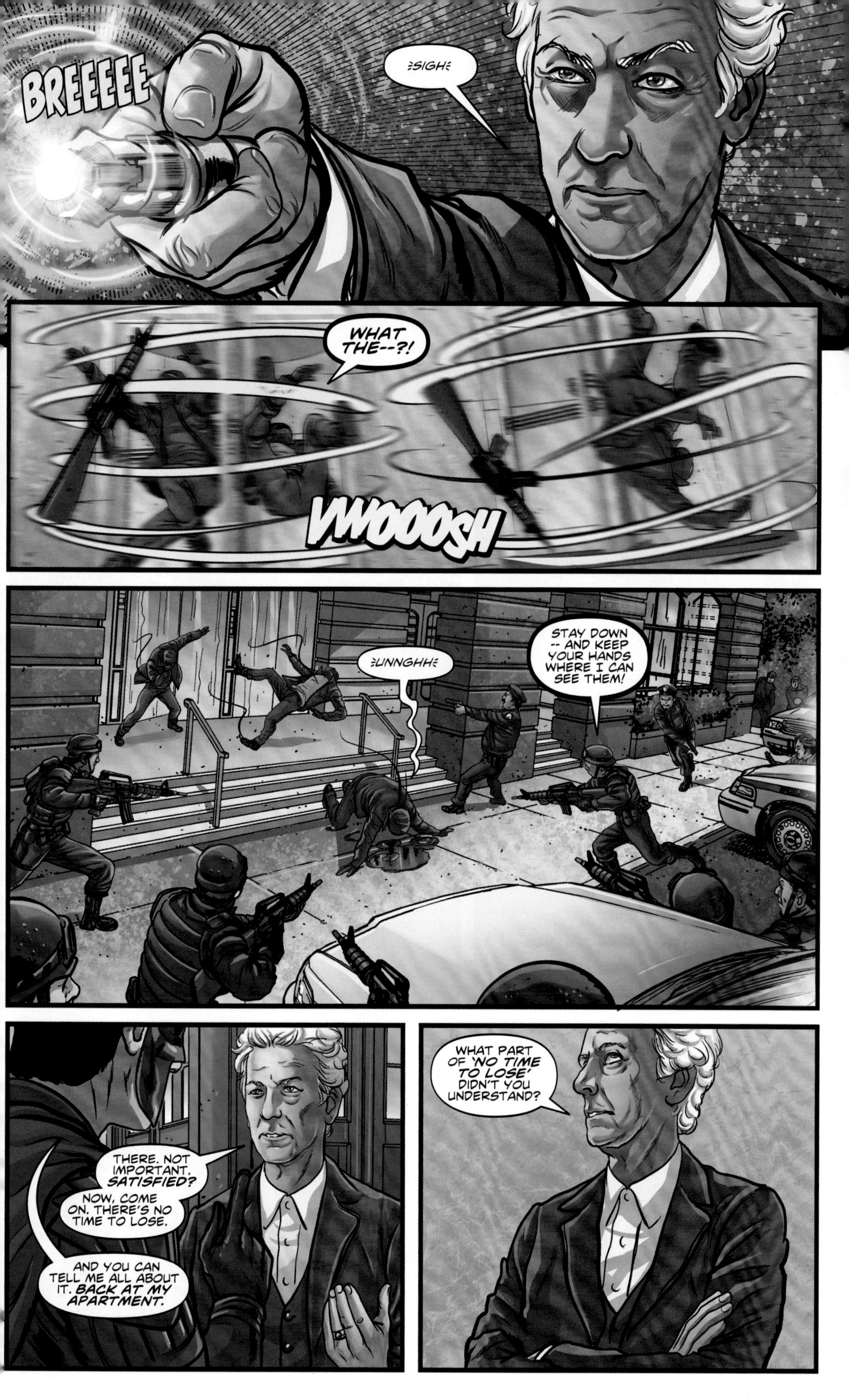
BREEEEE
SIGH
WHAT THE--?!
VWOOOSH
UNNGHH
STAY DOWN -- AND KEEP YOUR HANDS WHERE I CAN SEE THEM!
THERE. NOT IMPORTANT. SATISFIED?
NOW, COME ON. THERE'S NO TIME TO LOSE.
AND YOU CAN TELL ME ALL ABOUT IT. BACK AT MY APARTMENT.
WHAT PART OF 'NO TIME TO LOSE' DIDN'T YOU UNDERSTAND?

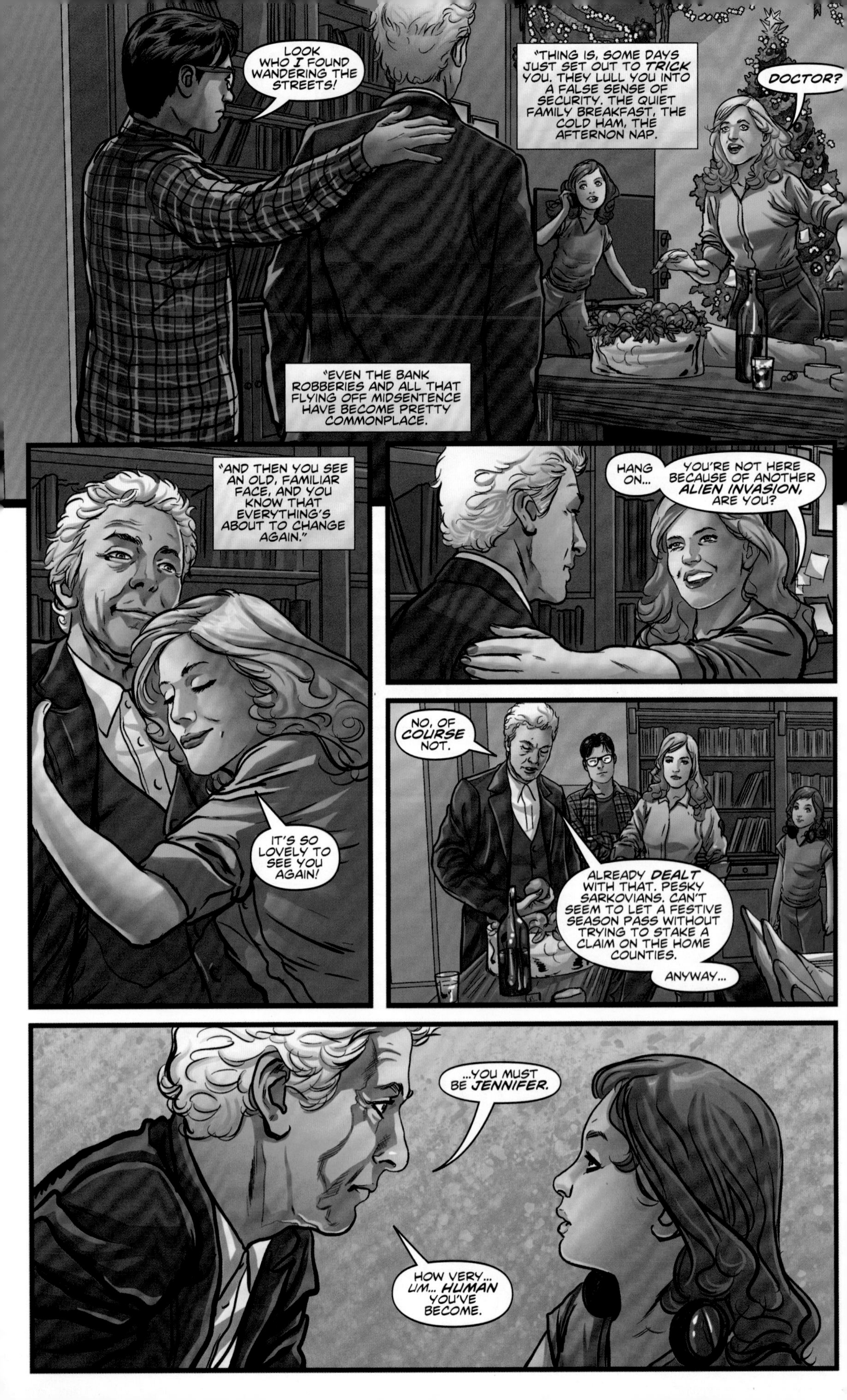
LOOK WHO *I* FOUND WANDERING THE STREETS!
"THING IS, SOME DAYS JUST SET OUT TO *TRICK* YOU. THEY LULL YOU INTO A FALSE SENSE OF SECURITY. THE QUIET FAMILY BREAKFAST, THE COLD HAM, THE AFTERNON NAP.
DOCTOR?
"EVEN THE BANK ROBBERIES AND ALL THAT FLYING OFF MIDSENTENCE HAVE BECOME PRETTY COMMONPLACE.
"AND THEN YOU SEE AN OLD, FAMILIAR FACE, AND YOU KNOW THAT EVERYTHING'S ABOUT TO CHANGE AGAIN."
IT'S SO LOVELY TO SEE YOU AGAIN!
HANG ON...
YOU'RE NOT HERE BECAUSE OF ANOTHER *ALIEN INVASION,* ARE YOU?
NO, OF *COURSE* NOT.
ALREADY *DEALT* WITH THAT. PESKY SARKOVIANS. CAN'T SEEM TO LET A FESTIVE SEASON PASS WITHOUT TRYING TO STAKE A CLAIM ON THE HOME COUNTIES.
ANYWAY...
...YOU MUST BE *JENNIFER.*
HOW VERY... UM... *HUMAN* YOU'VE BECOME.

SO, WHY *ARE* YOU HERE, DOCTOR? I MEAN, I KNOW FROM THE FACT WE HAVEN'T SEEN YOU FOR *EIGHT YEARS* THAT THIS CAN'T BE JUST A *SOCIAL* CALL.

I NEED TO *BORROW* YOUR STEPDAD FOR A LITTLE WHILE. JUST A QUICK WHIZZ TO THE OTHER SIDE OF THE GALAXY AND BACK. I'LL HAVE HIM HOME BEFORE TEATIME. PROMISE.

NO. HE PROMISED WE COULD HAVE A GAME OF POKÉMON LATER. IT'S *CHRISTMAS* AND HE'S STAYING AT *HOME.*

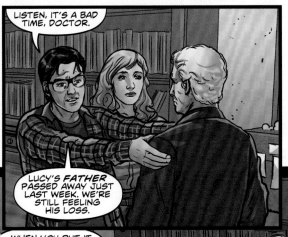

LISTEN, IT'S A BAD TIME, DOCTOR.

LUCY'S *FATHER* PASSED AWAY JUST LAST WEEK. WE'RE STILL FEELING HIS LOSS.

THE UNIVERSE DOESN'T WAIT FOR A *GOOD* TIME, GRANT. I NEED YOUR HELP. IT'S ALL AT RISK -- TIME, SPACE, *REALITY...*

I NEED YOU TO HELP ME FIND THE *OTHER* THREE CRYSTALS. WE CAN USE THE ONE *INSIDE* OF YOU TO TRACK THEM DOWN.

EVERYTHING DEPENDS ON IT.

...WHEN YOU PUT IT LIKE *THAT,* I DON'T SUPPOSE I HAVE A CHOICE.

BUT THERE'S A *CONDITION.*

LUCY AND JENNIFER COME WITH US. I'M NOT GOING WITHOUT THEM.

YOU REALLY *DO* HAVE A THING ABOUT GETTING YOUR WAY, DON'T YOU?

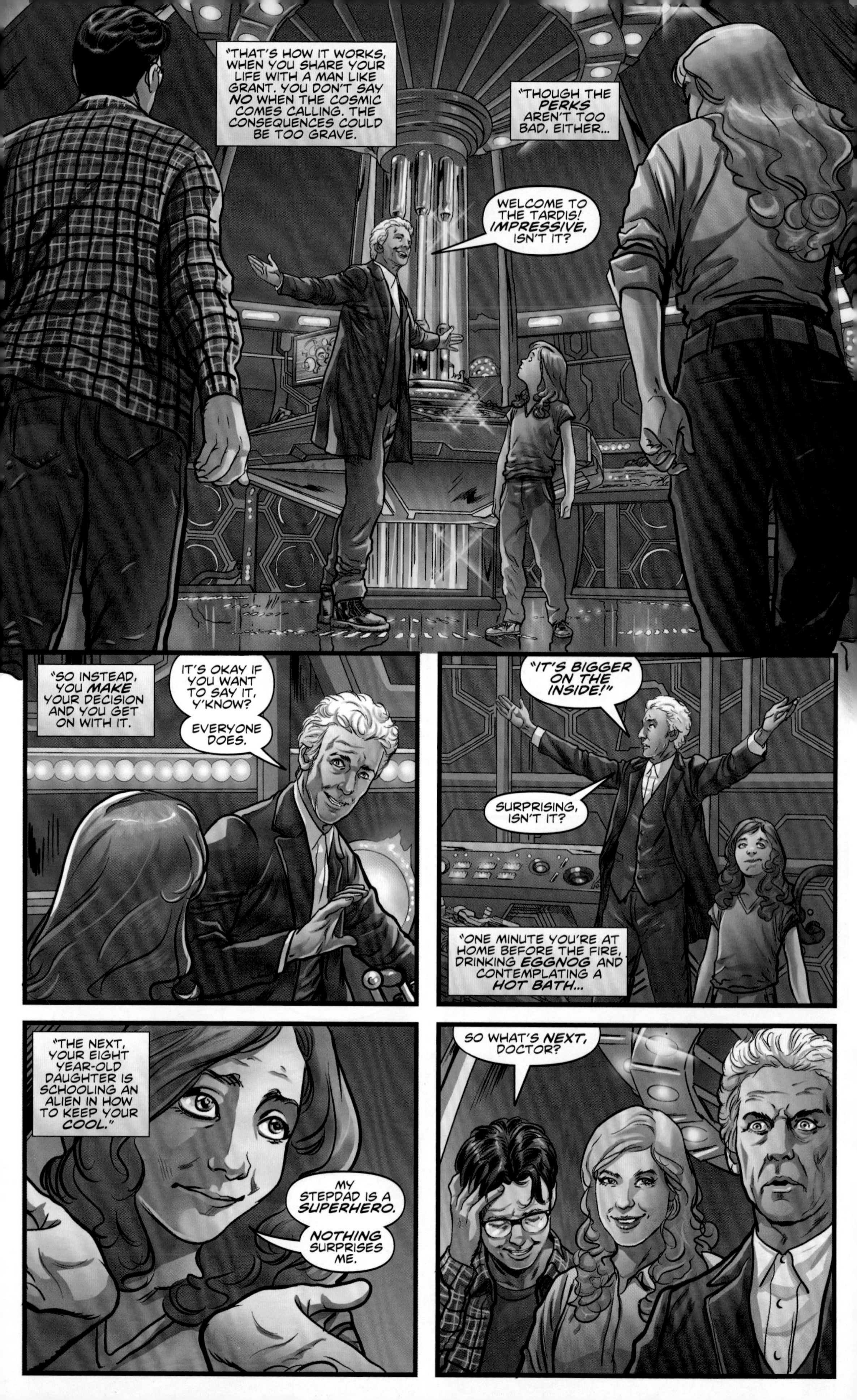
"THAT'S HOW IT WORKS, WHEN YOU SHARE YOUR LIFE WITH A MAN LIKE GRANT. YOU DON'T SAY NO WHEN THE COSMIC COMES CALLING. THE CONSEQUENCES COULD BE TOO GRAVE.
"THOUGH THE PERKS AREN'T TOO BAD, EITHER...
WELCOME TO THE TARDIS! IMPRESSIVE, ISN'T IT?
"SO INSTEAD, YOU MAKE YOUR DECISION AND YOU GET ON WITH IT.
IT'S OKAY IF YOU WANT TO SAY IT, Y'KNOW?
EVERYONE DOES.
"IT'S BIGGER ON THE INSIDE!"
SURPRISING, ISN'T IT?
"ONE MINUTE YOU'RE AT HOME BEFORE THE FIRE, DRINKING EGGNOG AND CONTEMPLATING A HOT BATH...
"THE NEXT, YOUR EIGHT YEAR-OLD DAUGHTER IS SCHOOLING AN ALIEN IN HOW TO KEEP YOUR COOL."
MY STEPDAD IS A SUPERHERO.
NOTHING SURPRISES ME.
SO WHAT'S NEXT, DOCTOR?

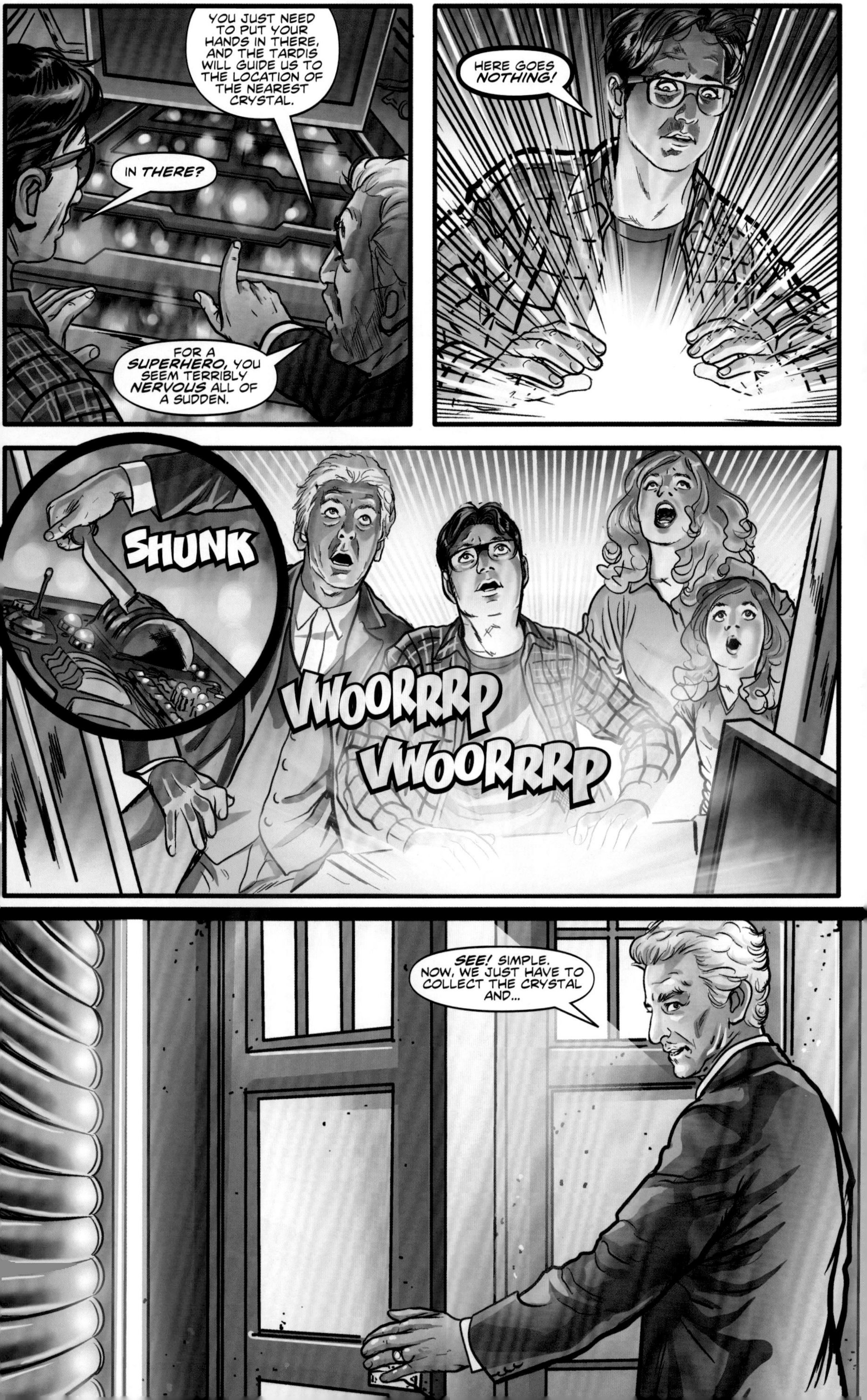
YOU JUST NEED TO PUT YOUR HANDS IN THERE, AND THE TARDIS WILL GUIDE US TO THE LOCATION OF THE NEAREST CRYSTAL.
IN THERE?
FOR A SUPERHERO, YOU SEEM TERRIBLY NERVOUS ALL OF A SUDDEN.
HERE GOES NOTHING!
SHUNK
VWOORRRP
VWOORRRP
SEE! SIMPLE. NOW, WE JUST HAVE TO COLLECT THE CRYSTAL AND...

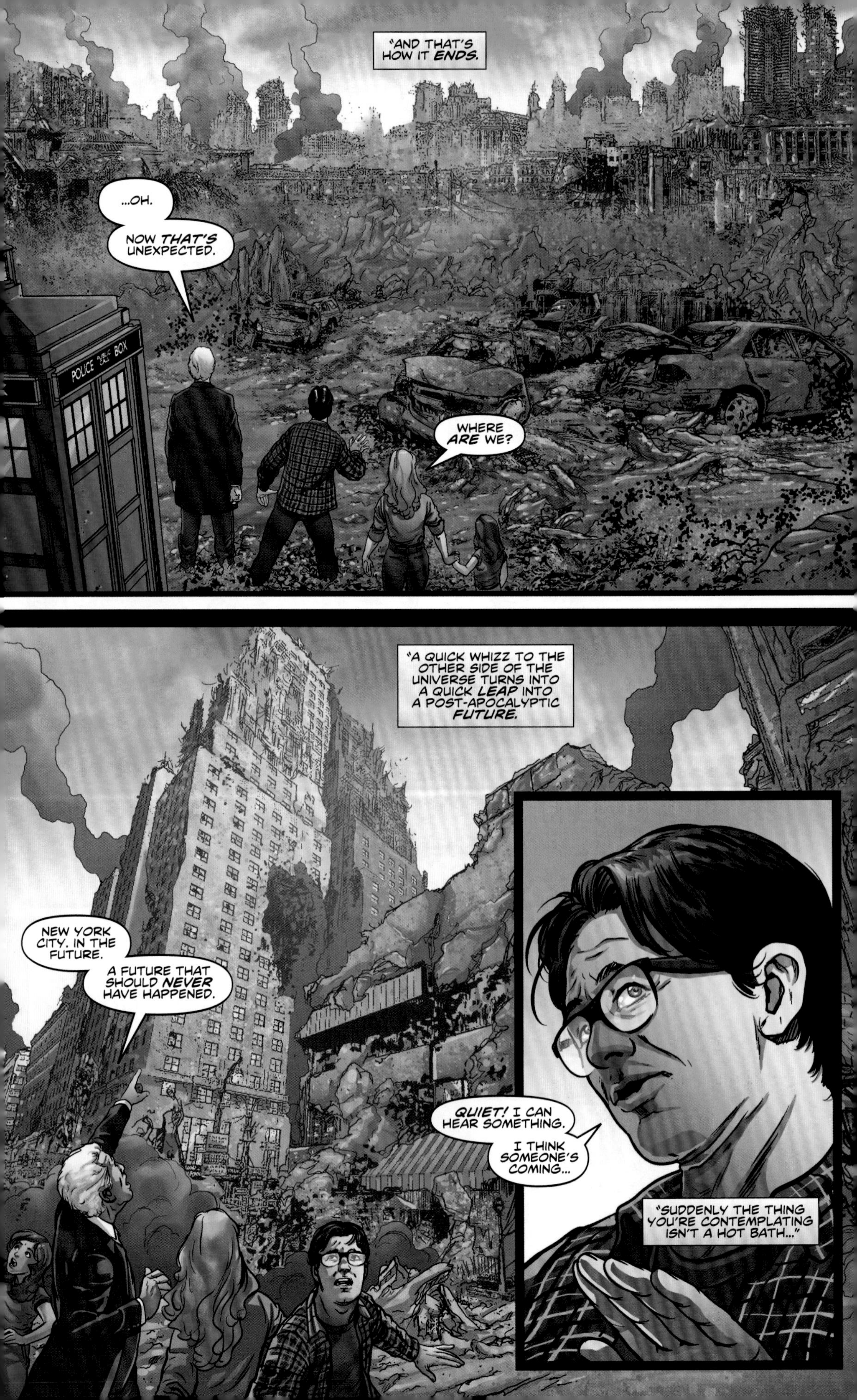
"AND THAT'S HOW IT *ENDS.*
...OH.
NOW *THAT'S* UNEXPECTED.
POLICE PUBLIC CALL BOX
WHERE *ARE* WE?
"A QUICK WHIZZ TO THE OTHER SIDE OF THE UNIVERSE TURNS INTO A QUICK *LEAP* INTO A POST-APOCALYPTIC *FUTURE.*
NEW YORK CITY. IN THE FUTURE.
A FUTURE THAT SHOULD *NEVER* HAVE HAPPENED.
QUIET! I CAN HEAR SOMETHING.
I THINK SOMEONE'S COMING...
"SUDDENLY THE THING YOU'RE CONTEMPLATING ISN'T A HOT BATH..."

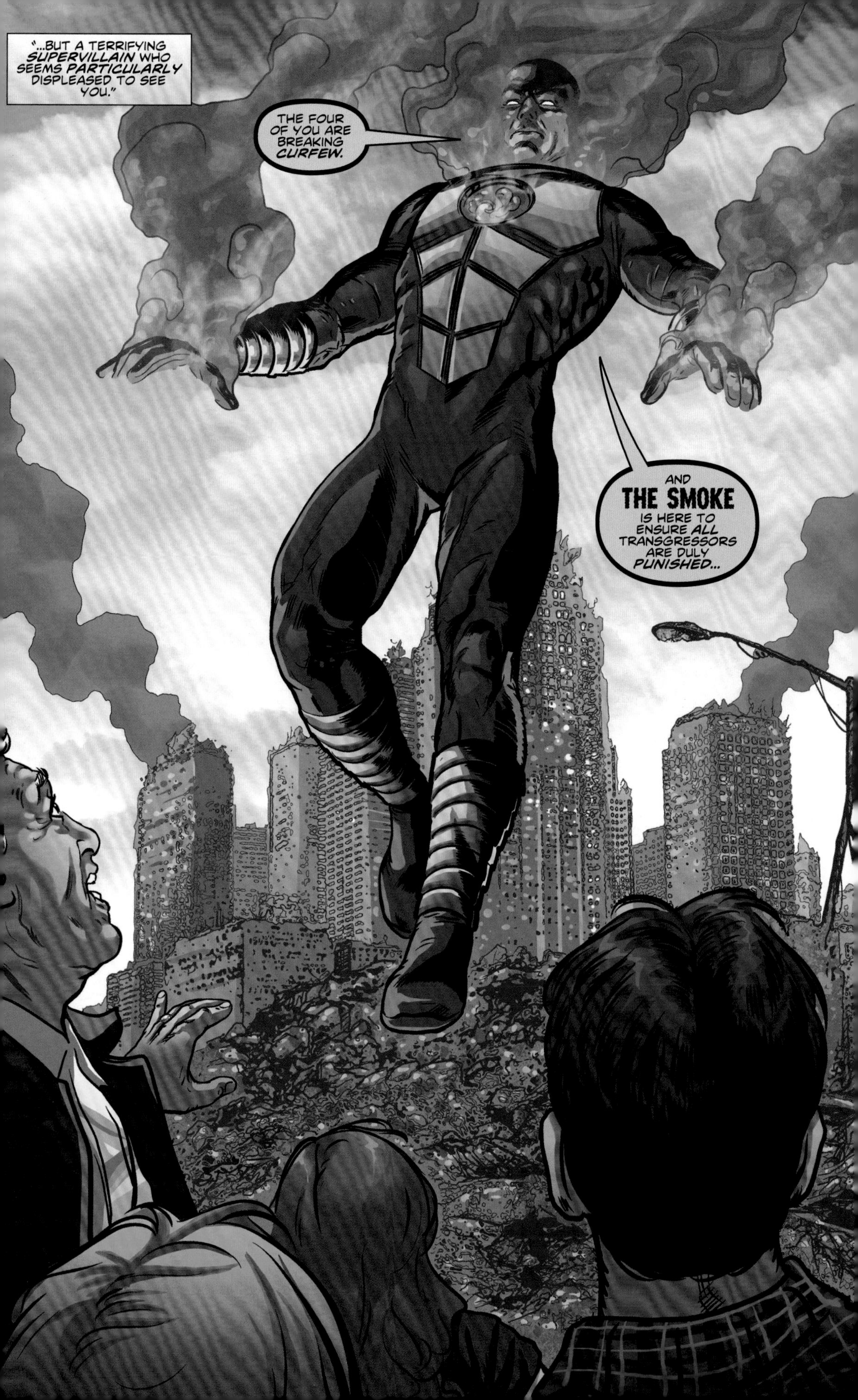
"...BUT A TERRIFYING SUPERVILLAIN WHO SEEMS PARTICULARLY DISPLEASED TO SEE YOU."
THE FOUR OF YOU ARE BREAKING CURFEW.
AND THE SMOKE IS HERE TO ENSURE ALL TRANSGRESSORS ARE DULY PUNISHED...

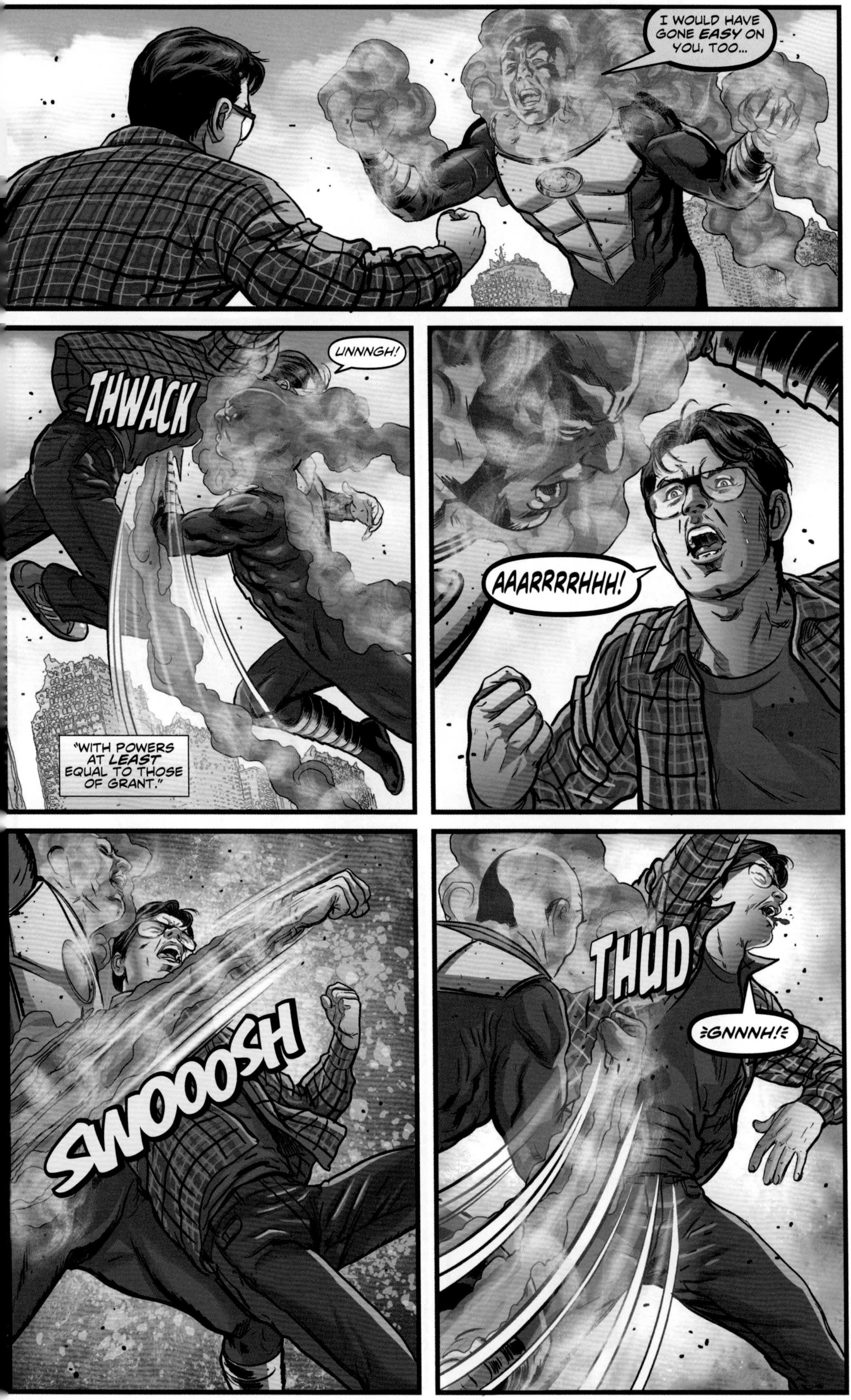
I WOULD HAVE GONE EASY ON YOU, TOO...
UNNNGH!
THWACK
"WITH POWERS AT LEAST EQUAL TO THOSE OF GRANT."
AAARRRRHHH!
SWOOOSH
THUD
GNNNH!

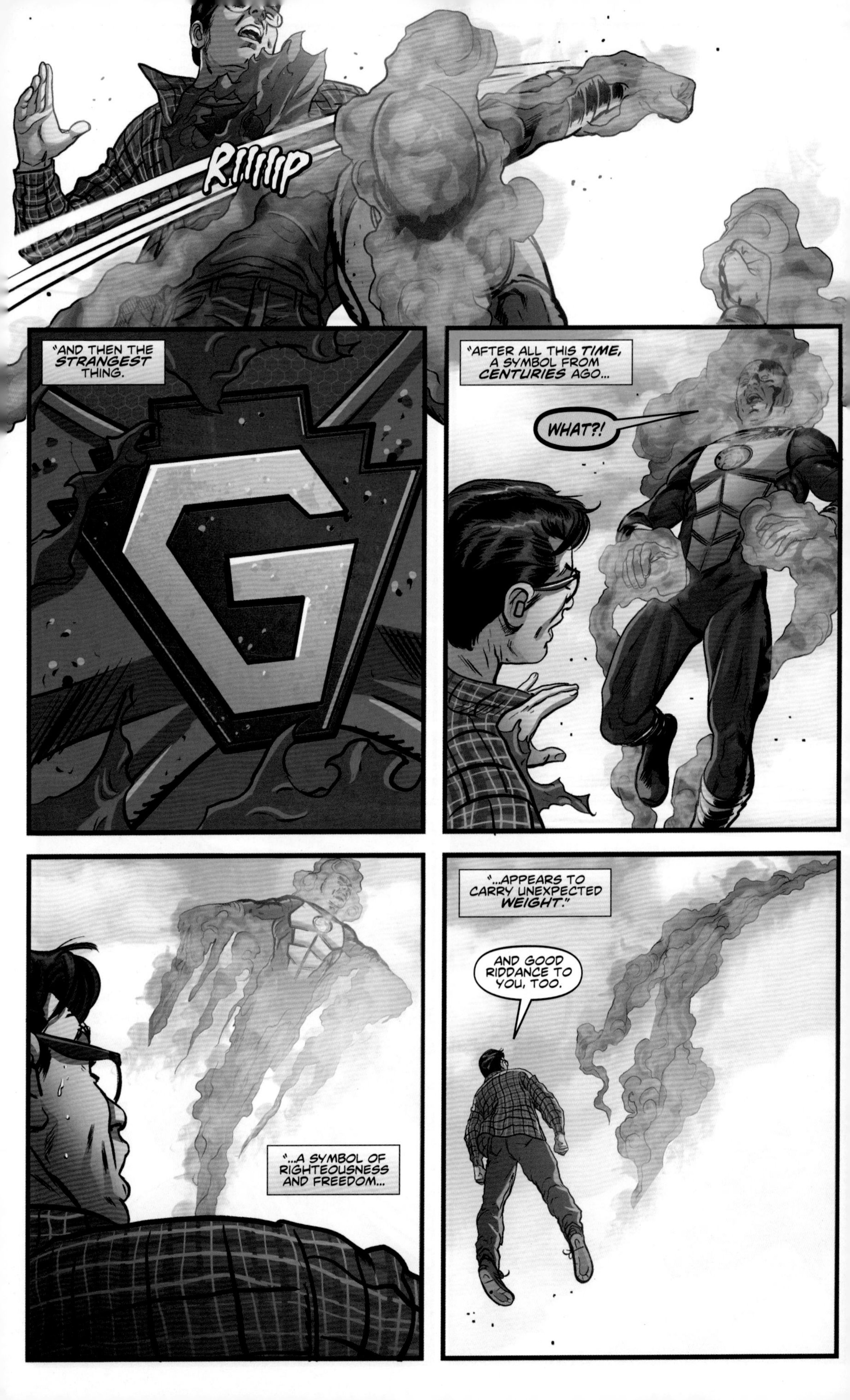
RIIIIP
"AND THEN THE STRANGEST THING.
"AFTER ALL THIS TIME, A SYMBOL FROM CENTURIES AGO...
WHAT?!
"...A SYMBOL OF RIGHTEOUSNESS AND FREEDOM...
"...APPEARS TO CARRY UNEXPECTED WEIGHT."
AND GOOD RIDDANCE TO YOU, TOO.

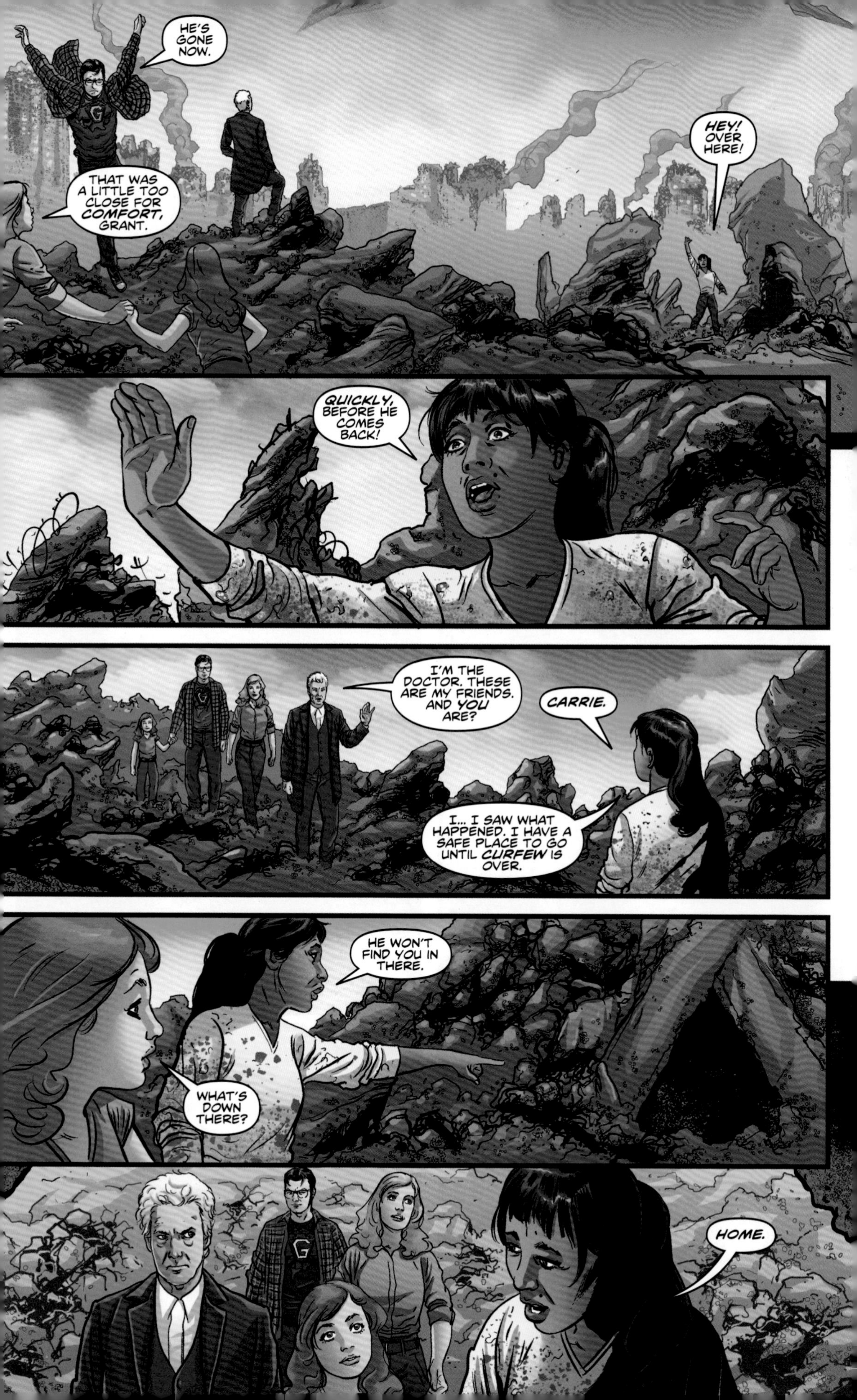
HE'S GONE NOW.
THAT WAS A LITTLE TOO CLOSE FOR COMFORT, GRANT.
HEY! OVER HERE!
QUICKLY, BEFORE HE COMES BACK!
I'M THE DOCTOR. THESE ARE MY FRIENDS. AND YOU ARE?
CARRIE.
I... I SAW WHAT HAPPENED. I HAVE A SAFE PLACE TO GO UNTIL CURFEW IS OVER.
HE WON'T FIND YOU IN THERE.
WHAT'S DOWN THERE?
HOME.

COME ON, THIS WAY.

THESE ARE THE *DISPOSSESSED*, THE PEOPLE WHO LOST THEIR HOMES DURING THE CONFLICT.

"THE THINGS I SEE DOWN HERE...

"IT'S LIKE THE *WORST* IMPOVERISHMENT OF THE 21ST CENTURY, BUT *RIGHT HERE*, IN THE HEART OF NYC, LIKE PEOPLE ARE LIVING IN THE AFTERMATH OF A GREAT DISASTER OR *WAR*.

THEY COME HERE TO SHELTER DURING THE CURFEW. TO AVOID *PUNISHMENT* BY THE SMOKE.

THEY HAVE NOWHERE ELSE TO GO.

THROUGH HERE. I'LL FETCH YOU SOMETHING TO DRINK.

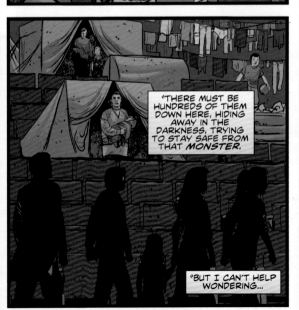

"THERE MUST BE HUNDREDS OF THEM DOWN HERE, HIDING AWAY IN THE DARKNESS, TRYING TO STAY SAFE FROM THAT *MONSTER*.

"BUT I CAN'T HELP WONDERING...

"WHAT HAPPENED TO EVERYONE *ELSE*?"

HERE WE ARE. I KNOW IT'S NOT *MUCH* BUT MAKE YOURSELVES COMFORTABLE.

COFFEE?

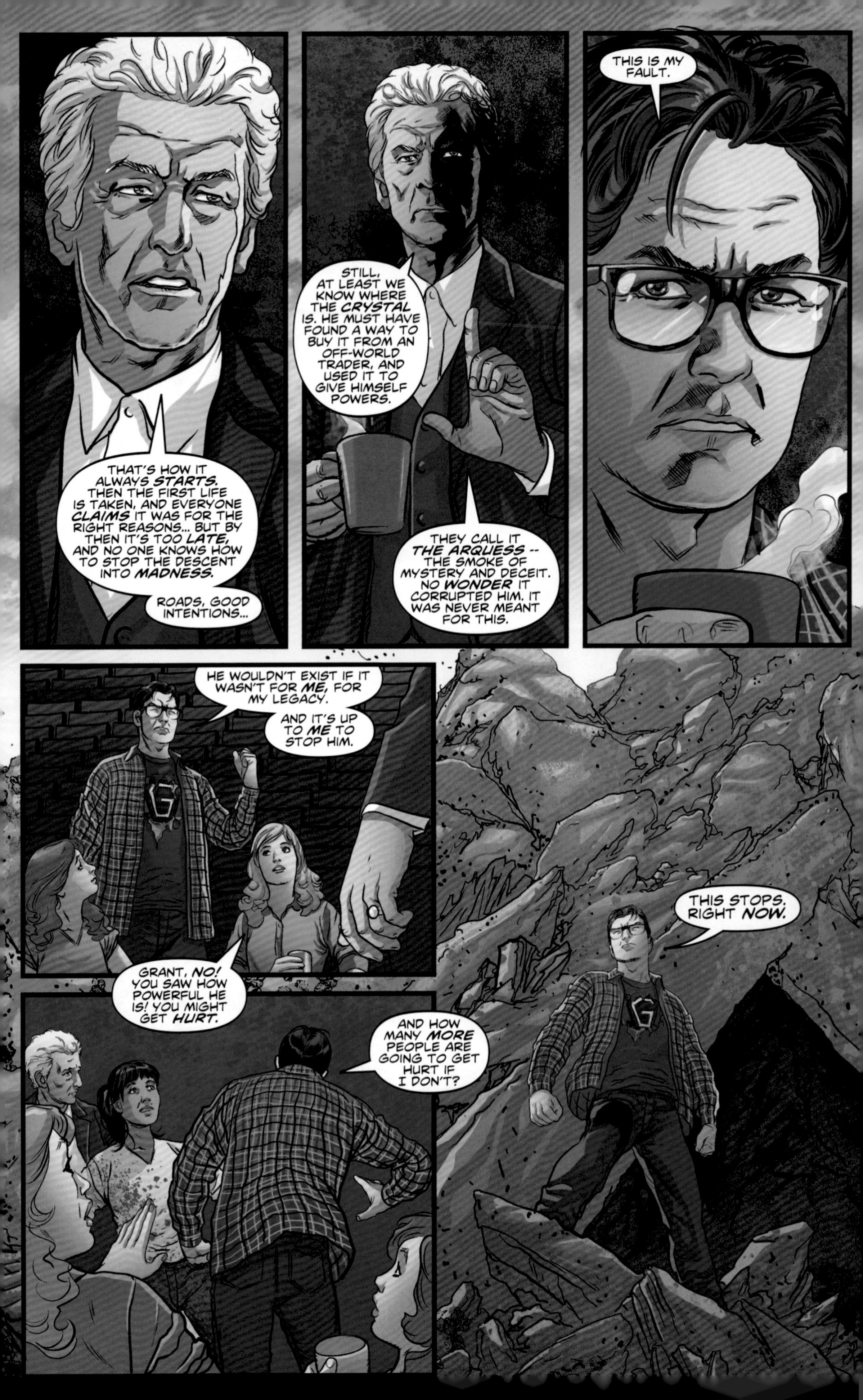
THAT'S HOW IT ALWAYS STARTS. THEN THE FIRST LIFE IS TAKEN, AND EVERYONE CLAIMS IT WAS FOR THE RIGHT REASONS... BUT BY THEN IT'S TOO LATE, AND NO ONE KNOWS HOW TO STOP THE DESCENT INTO MADNESS.
ROADS, GOOD INTENTIONS...
STILL, AT LEAST WE KNOW WHERE THE CRYSTAL IS. HE MUST HAVE FOUND A WAY TO BUY IT FROM AN OFF-WORLD TRADER, AND USED IT TO GIVE HIMSELF POWERS.
THEY CALL IT THE ARQUESS -- THE SMOKE OF MYSTERY AND DECEIT. NO WONDER IT CORRUPTED HIM. IT WAS NEVER MEANT FOR THIS.
THIS IS MY FAULT.
HE WOULDN'T EXIST IF IT WASN'T FOR ME, FOR MY LEGACY.
AND IT'S UP TO ME TO STOP HIM.
GRANT, NO! YOU SAW HOW POWERFUL HE IS! YOU MIGHT GET HURT.
AND HOW MANY MORE PEOPLE ARE GOING TO GET HURT IF I DON'T?
THIS STOPS, RIGHT NOW.

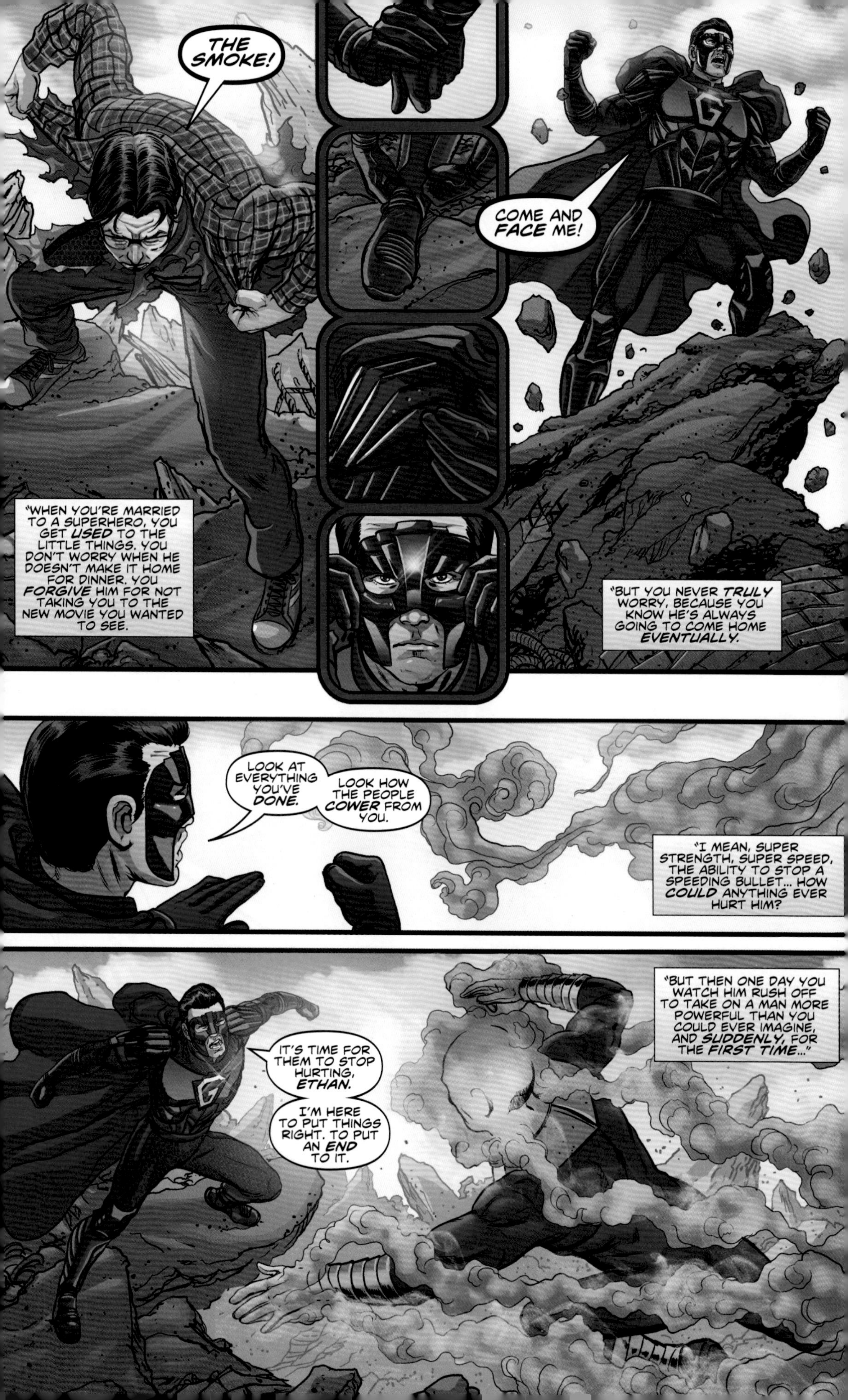
THE SMOKE!
COME AND FACE ME!
"WHEN YOU'RE MARRIED TO A SUPERHERO, YOU GET USED TO THE LITTLE THINGS. YOU DON'T WORRY WHEN HE DOESN'T MAKE IT HOME FOR DINNER. YOU FORGIVE HIM FOR NOT TAKING YOU TO THE NEW MOVIE YOU WANTED TO SEE.
"BUT YOU NEVER TRULY WORRY, BECAUSE YOU KNOW HE'S ALWAYS GOING TO COME HOME EVENTUALLY.
LOOK AT EVERYTHING YOU'VE DONE.
LOOK HOW THE PEOPLE COWER FROM YOU.
"I MEAN, SUPER STRENGTH, SUPER SPEED, THE ABILITY TO STOP A SPEEDING BULLET... HOW COULD ANYTHING EVER HURT HIM?
IT'S TIME FOR THEM TO STOP HURTING, ETHAN.
I'M HERE TO PUT THINGS RIGHT. TO PUT AN END TO IT.
"BUT THEN ONE DAY YOU WATCH HIM RUSH OFF TO TAKE ON A MAN MORE POWERFUL THAN YOU COULD EVER IMAGINE, AND SUDDENLY, FOR THE FIRST TIME..."

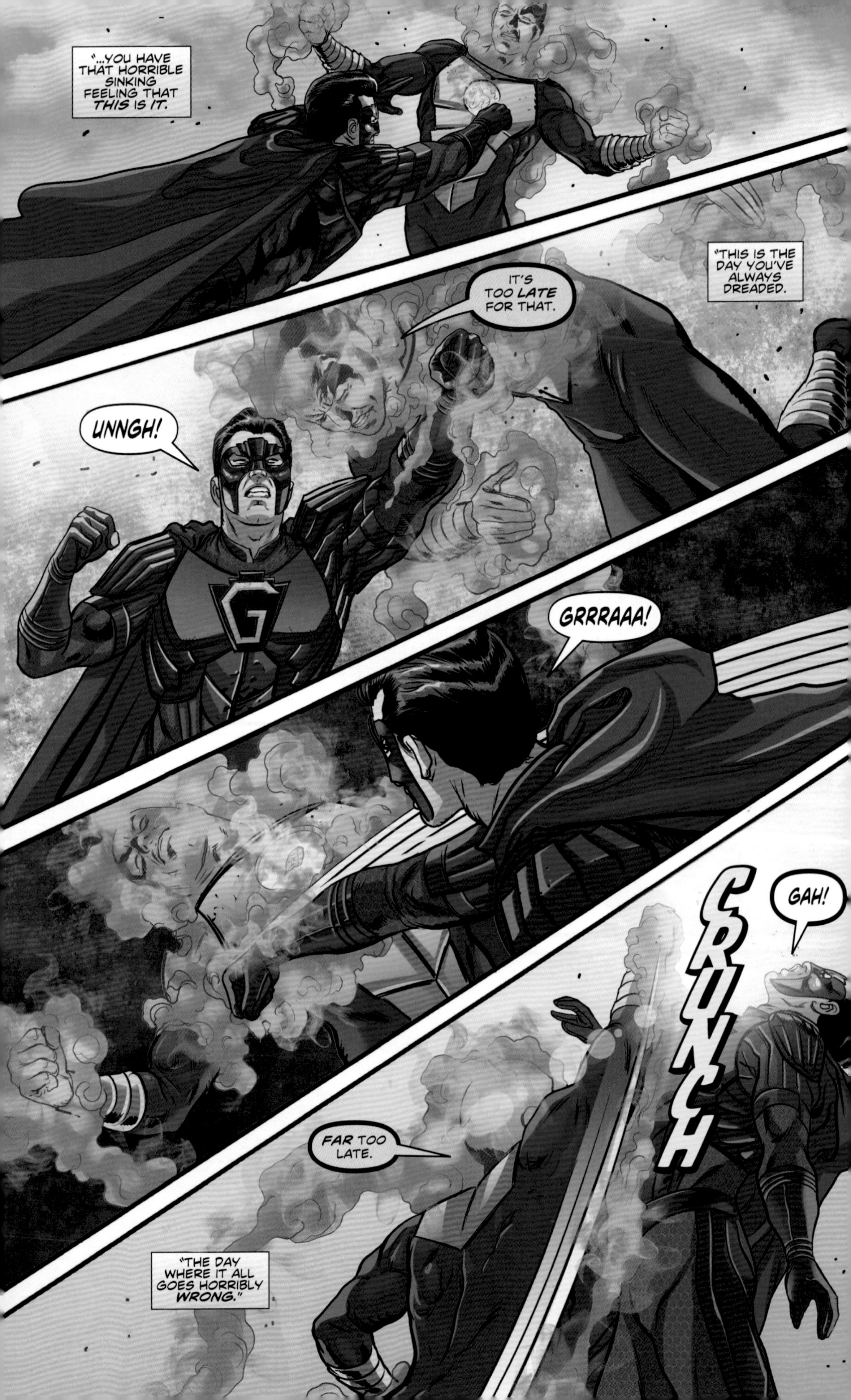
"...YOU HAVE THAT HORRIBLE SINKING FEELING THAT *THIS* IS *IT*.
"THIS IS THE DAY YOU'VE ALWAYS DREADED.
IT'S TOO *LATE* FOR THAT.
UNNGH!
GRRRAAA!
GAH!
CRUNCH
FAR TOO LATE.
"THE DAY WHERE IT ALL GOES HORRIBLY *WRONG*."

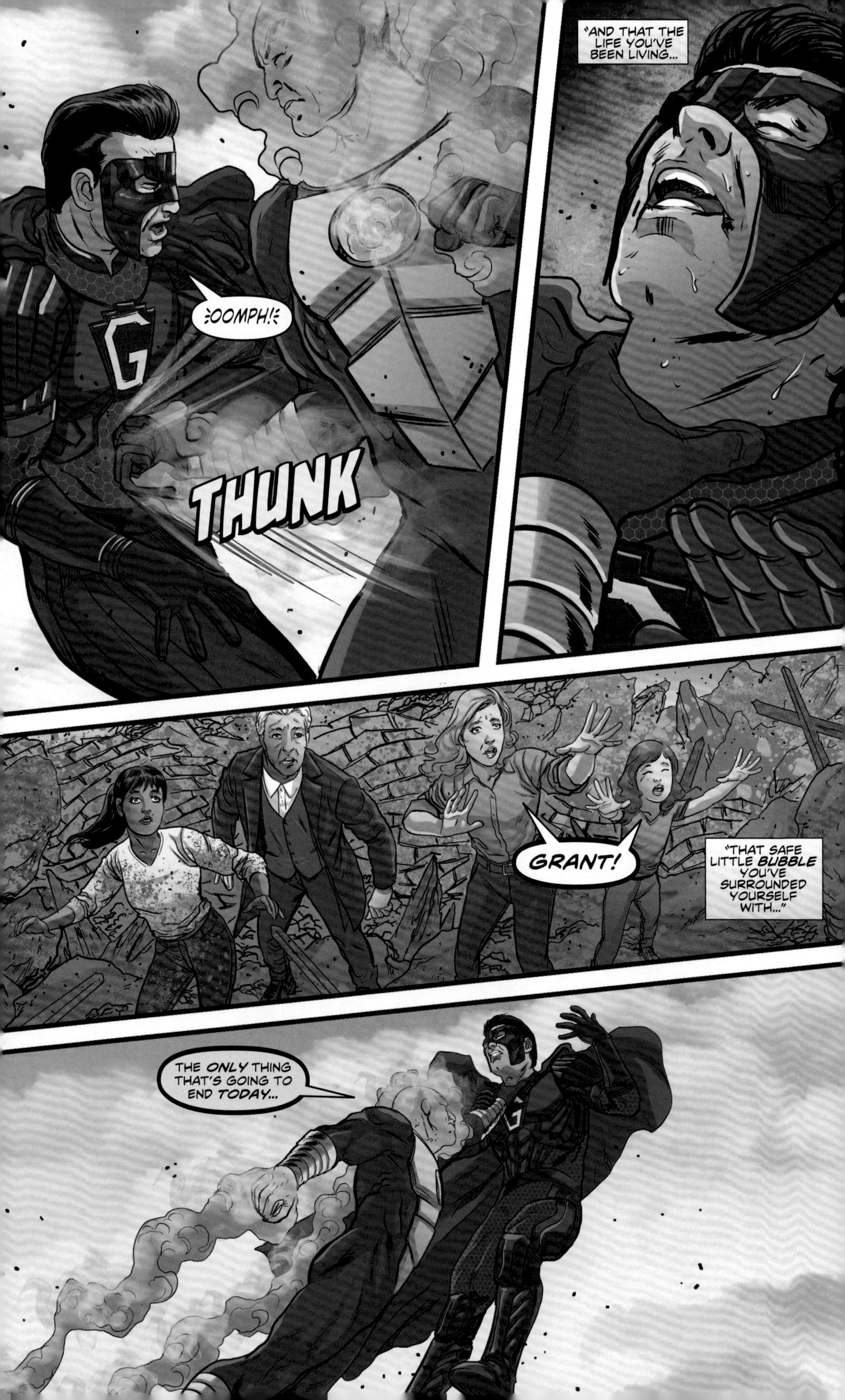
OOMPH!
THUNK
"AND THAT THE LIFE YOU'VE BEEN LIVING...
GRANT!
"THAT SAFE LITTLE BUBBLE YOU'VE SURROUNDED YOURSELF WITH..."
THE ONLY THING THAT'S GOING TO END TODAY...

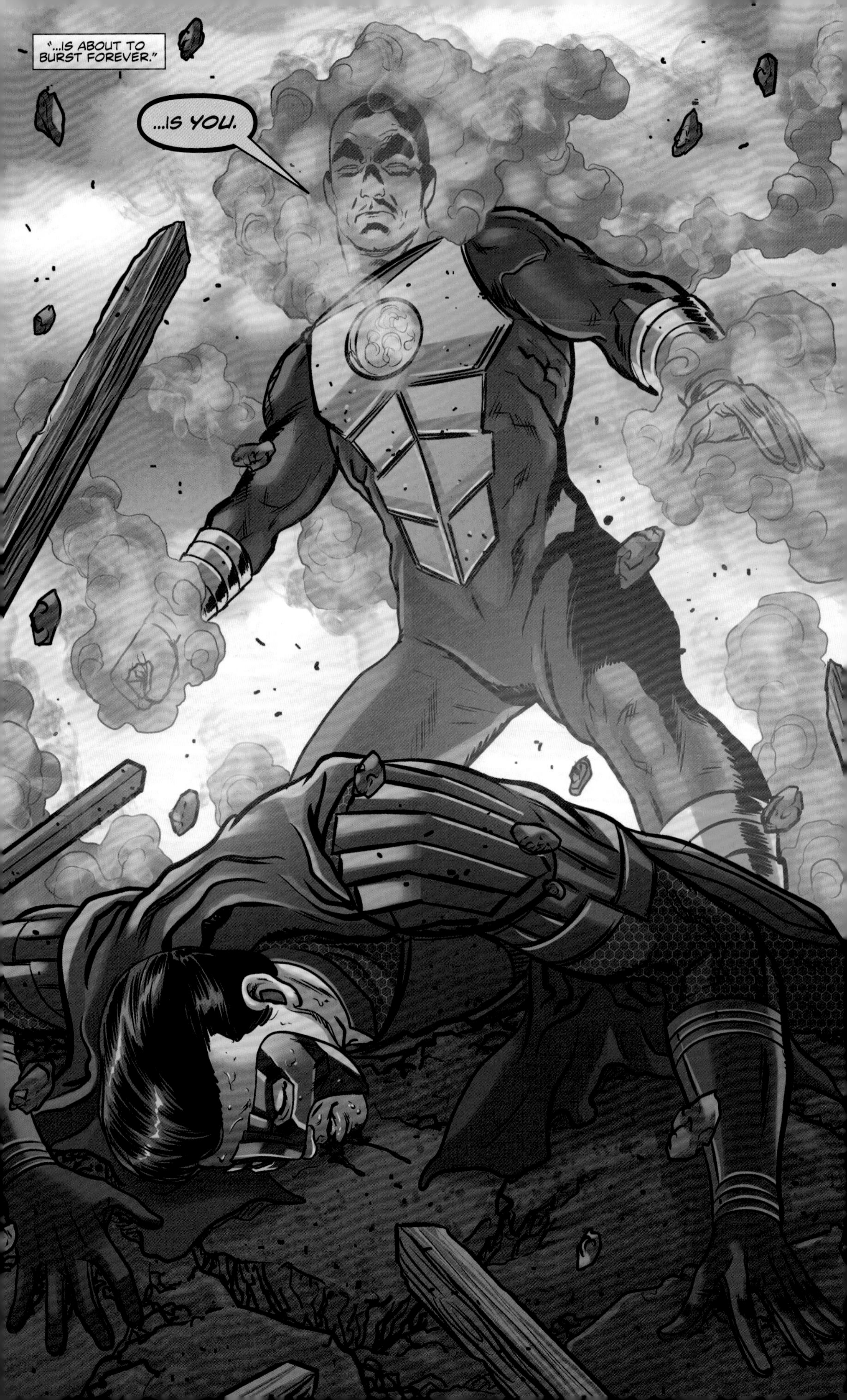
"...IS ABOUT TO BURST FOREVER."
...IS YOU.

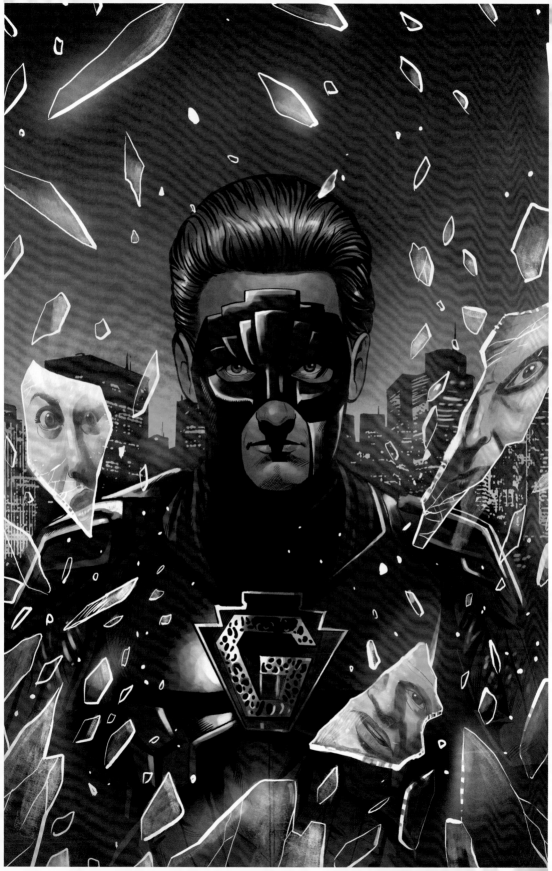

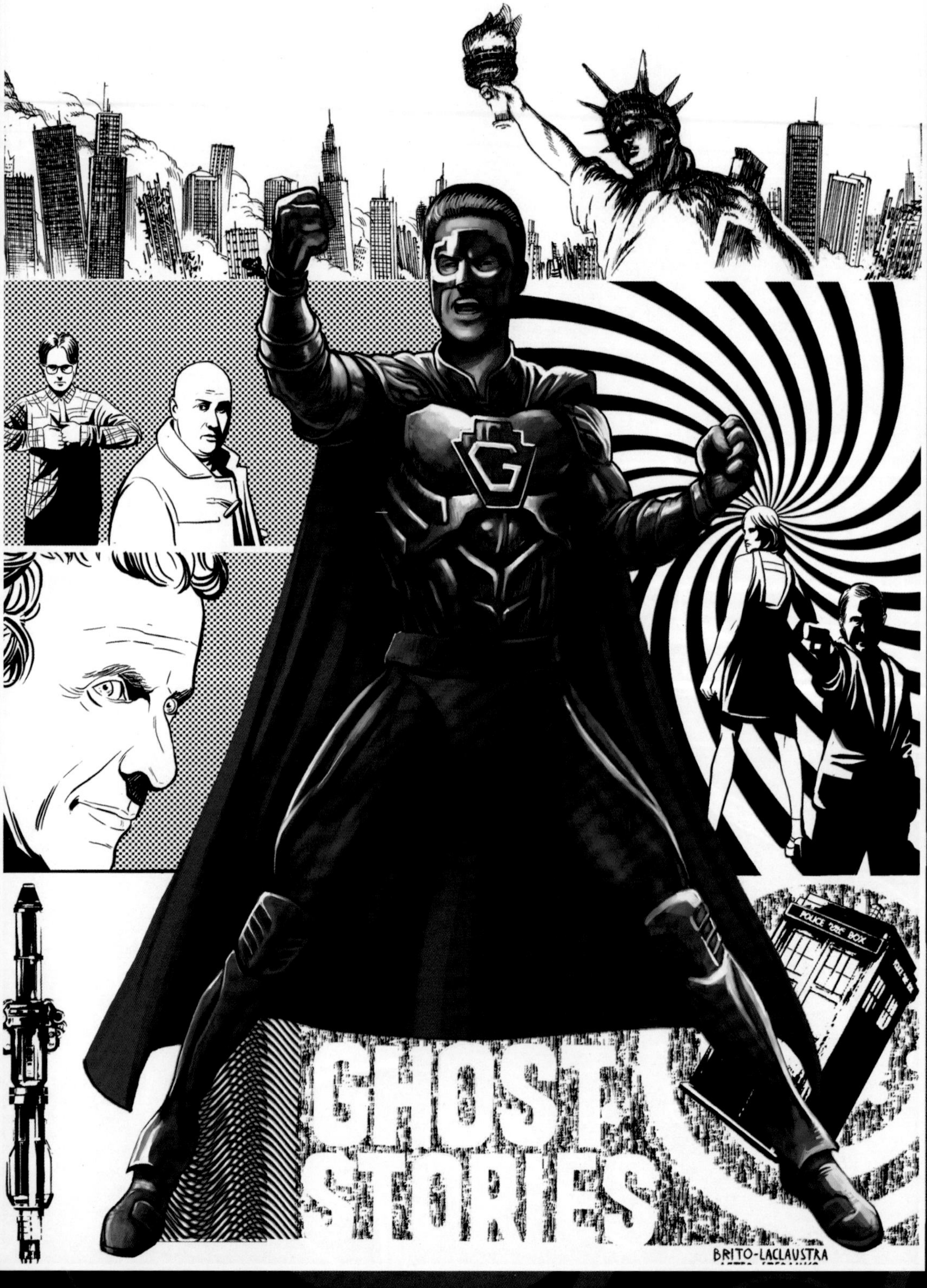
GHOST STORIES
BRITO-LACLAUSTRA

#2 Cover A: MARIANO LACLAUSTRA & PIER BRITO

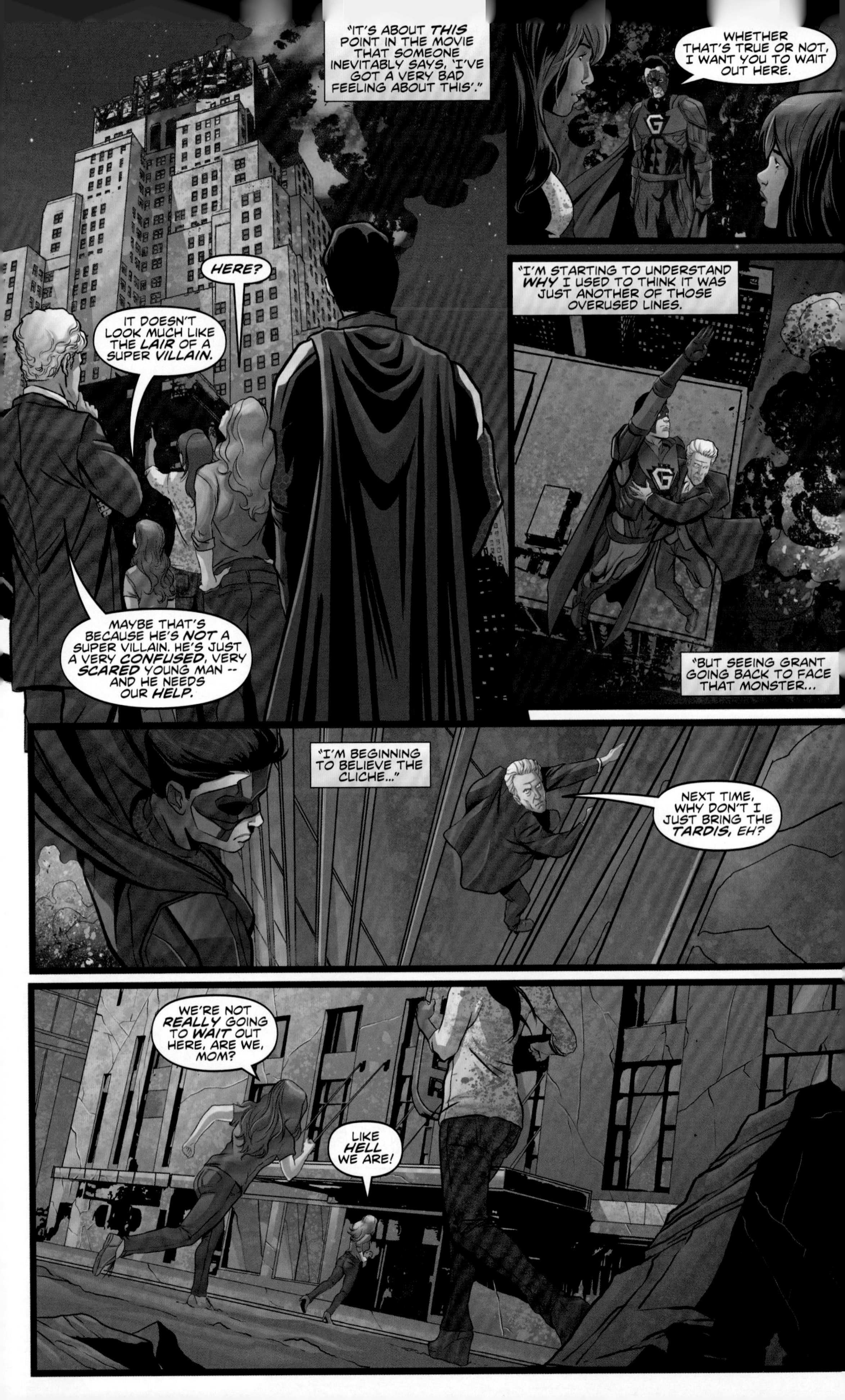
"IT'S ABOUT THIS POINT IN THE MOVIE THAT SOMEONE INEVITABLY SAYS, 'I'VE GOT A VERY BAD FEELING ABOUT THIS'."
HERE?
IT DOESN'T LOOK MUCH LIKE THE LAIR OF A SUPER VILLAIN.
MAYBE THAT'S BECAUSE HE'S NOT A SUPER VILLAIN. HE'S JUST A VERY CONFUSED, VERY SCARED YOUNG MAN -- AND HE NEEDS OUR HELP.
WHETHER THAT'S TRUE OR NOT, I WANT YOU TO WAIT OUT HERE.
"I'M STARTING TO UNDERSTAND WHY I USED TO THINK IT WAS JUST ANOTHER OF THOSE OVERUSED LINES.
"BUT SEEING GRANT GOING BACK TO FACE THAT MONSTER...
"I'M BEGINNING TO BELIEVE THE CLICHE..."
NEXT TIME, WHY DON'T I JUST BRING THE TARDIS, EH?
WE'RE NOT REALLY GOING TO WAIT OUT HERE, ARE WE, MOM?
LIKE HELL WE ARE!

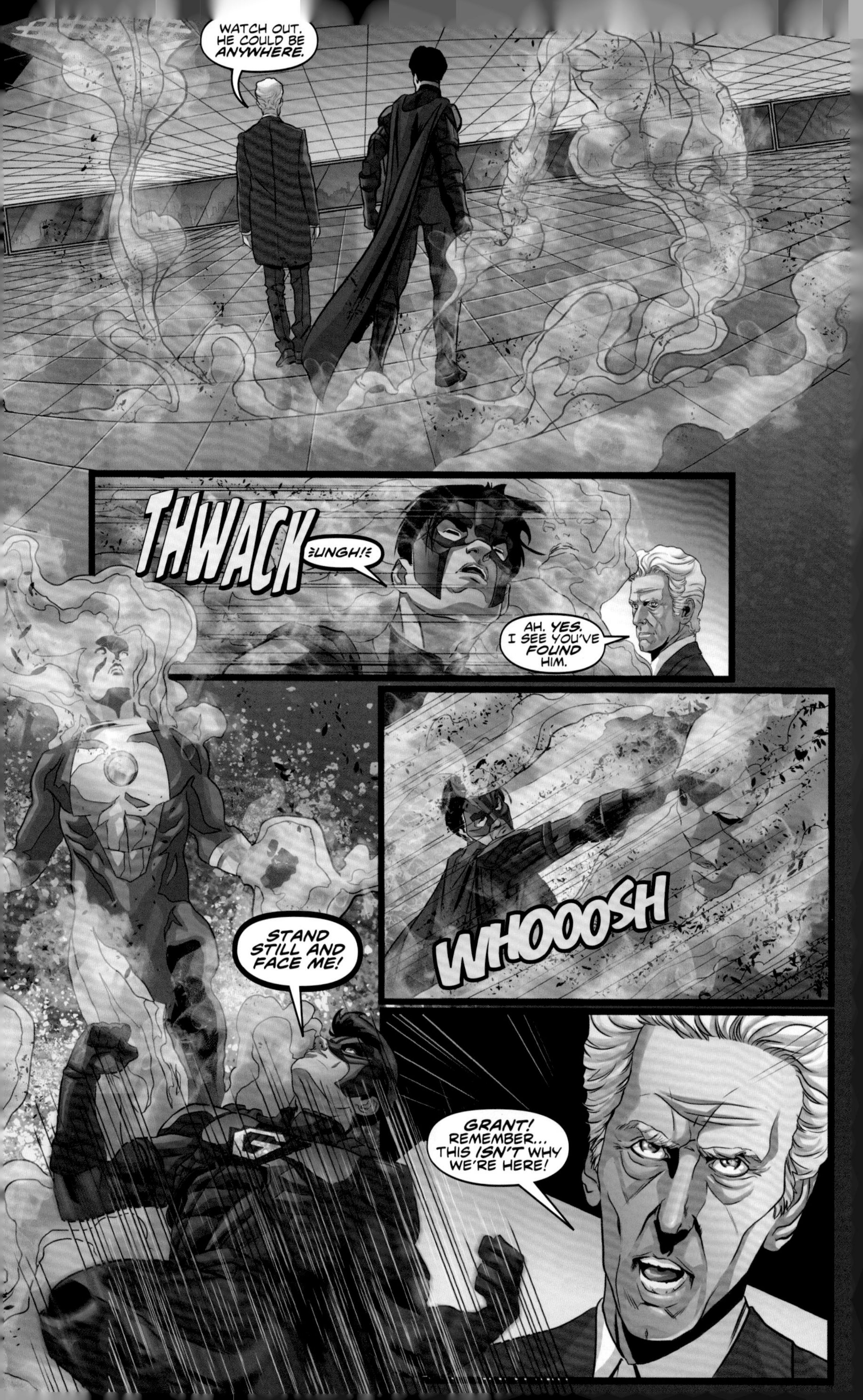
WATCH OUT. HE COULD BE ANYWHERE.
THWACK
UNGH!
AH. YES. I SEE YOU'VE FOUND HIM.
WHOOOSH
STAND STILL AND FACE ME!
GRANT! REMEMBER... THIS ISN'T WHY WE'RE HERE!

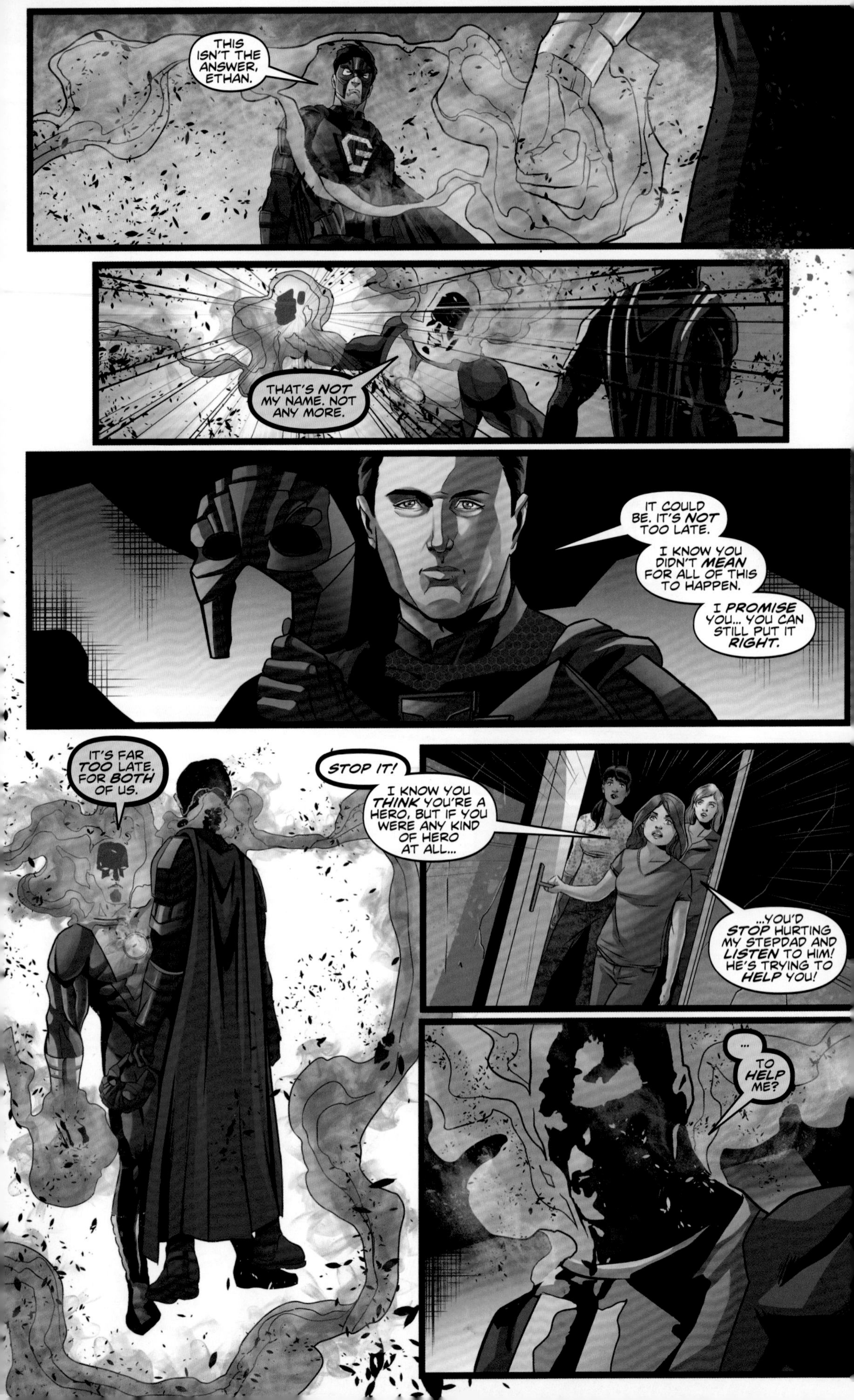

THIS ISN'T THE ANSWER, ETHAN.
THAT'S NOT MY NAME. NOT ANY MORE.
IT COULD BE. IT'S NOT TOO LATE.
I KNOW YOU DIDN'T MEAN FOR ALL OF THIS TO HAPPEN.
I PROMISE YOU... YOU CAN STILL PUT IT RIGHT.
IT'S FAR TOO LATE. FOR BOTH OF US.
STOP IT!
I KNOW YOU THINK YOU'RE A HERO, BUT IF YOU WERE ANY KIND OF HERO AT ALL...
...YOU'D STOP HURTING MY STEPDAD AND LISTEN TO HIM! HE'S TRYING TO HELP YOU!
... TO HELP ME?

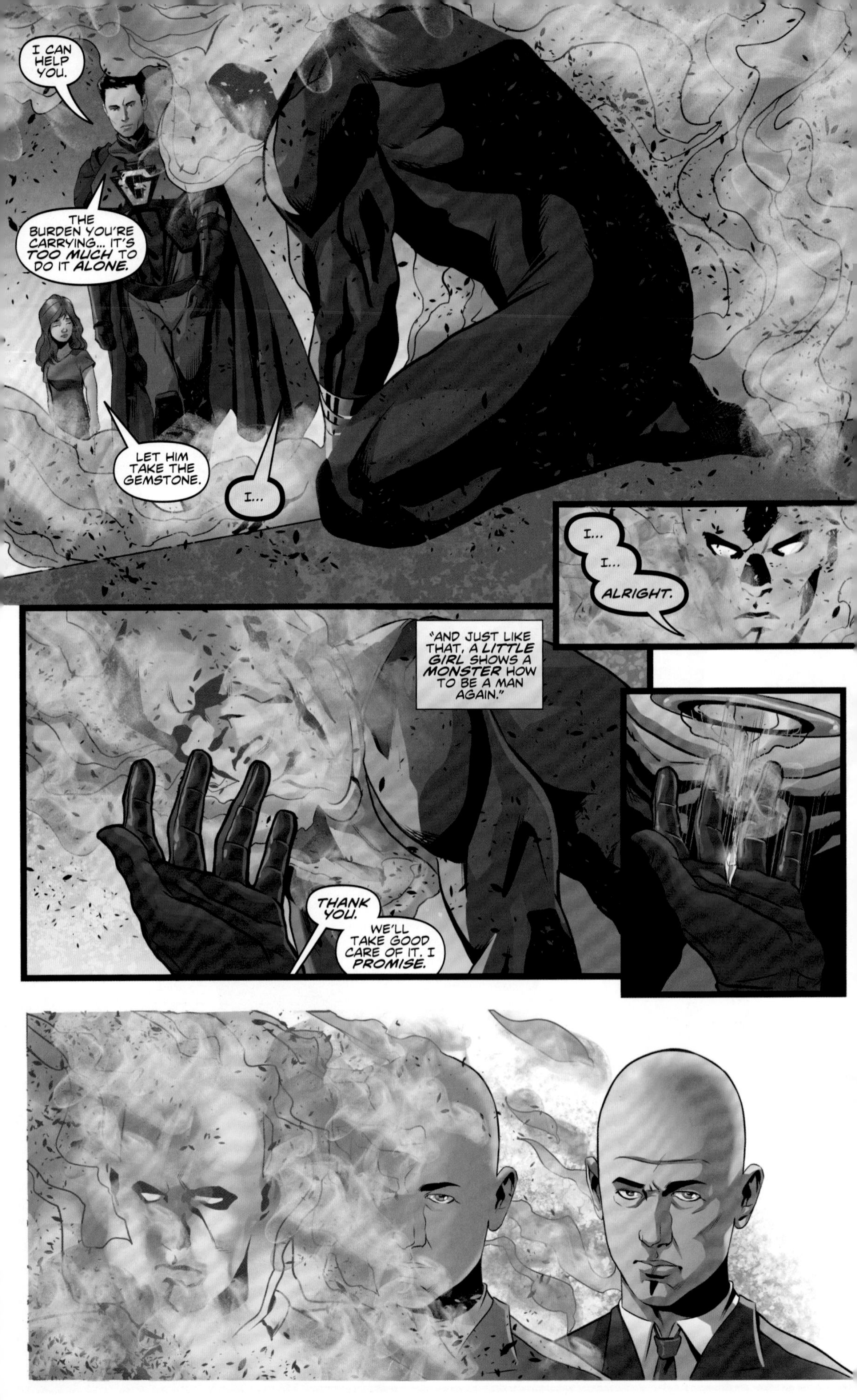
I CAN HELP YOU.
THE BURDEN YOU'RE CARRYING... IT'S TOO MUCH TO DO IT ALONE.
LET HIM TAKE THE GEMSTONE.
I...
I... I... ALRIGHT.
"AND JUST LIKE THAT, A LITTLE GIRL SHOWS A MONSTER HOW TO BE A MAN AGAIN."
THANK YOU.
WE'LL TAKE GOOD CARE OF IT. I PROMISE.

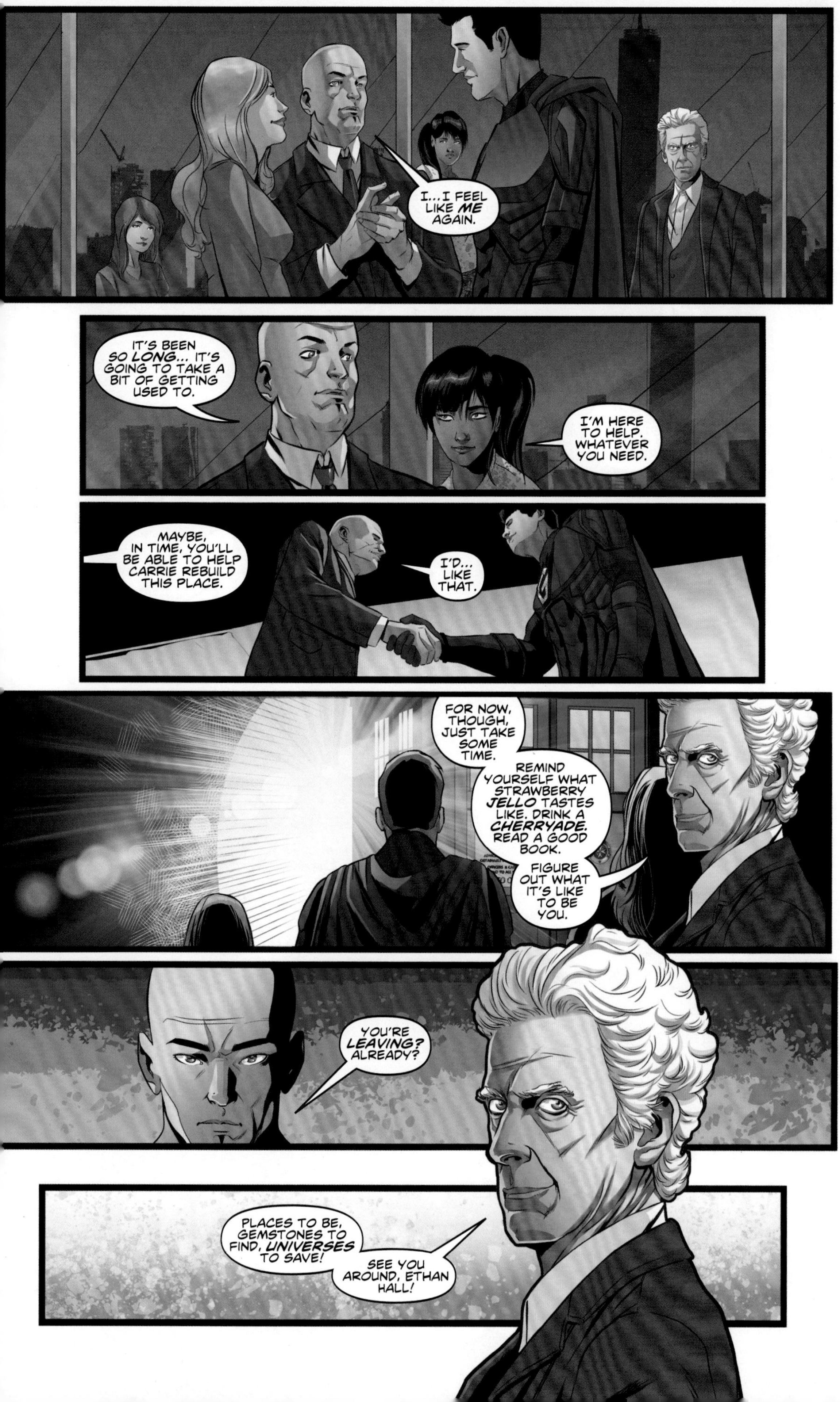
I... I FEEL LIKE ME AGAIN.
IT'S BEEN SO LONG... IT'S GOING TO TAKE A BIT OF GETTING USED TO.
I'M HERE TO HELP. WHATEVER YOU NEED.
MAYBE, IN TIME, YOU'LL BE ABLE TO HELP CARRIE REBUILD THIS PLACE.
I'D... LIKE THAT.
FOR NOW, THOUGH, JUST TAKE SOME TIME.
REMIND YOURSELF WHAT STRAWBERRY JELLO TASTES LIKE. DRINK A CHERRYADE. READ A GOOD BOOK.
FIGURE OUT WHAT IT'S LIKE TO BE YOU.
YOU'RE LEAVING? ALREADY?
PLACES TO BE, GEMSTONES TO FIND, UNIVERSES TO SAVE!
SEE YOU AROUND, ETHAN HALL!

"I WONDER HOW LONG HE'S BEEN DOING THIS. HE SEEMED SO CERTAIN THINGS WERE GOING TO WORK OUT IN THE END. HE EVEN SEEMS TO BE ENJOYING HIMSELF.
RIGHT-O! NO TIME FOR RESTING ON OUR LAURELS.
WE'VE GOT ANOTHER TWO GEMSTONES TO FIND BEFORE TEA!
"ALTHOUGH, ON REFLECTION, HE'S NOT THE ONLY ONE..."
HOLD ON TIGHT!
POLICE BOX
POLICE TELEPHONE
FREE
PUBLIC
PULL TO OPEN
VWOORRRP
VWOORRRP

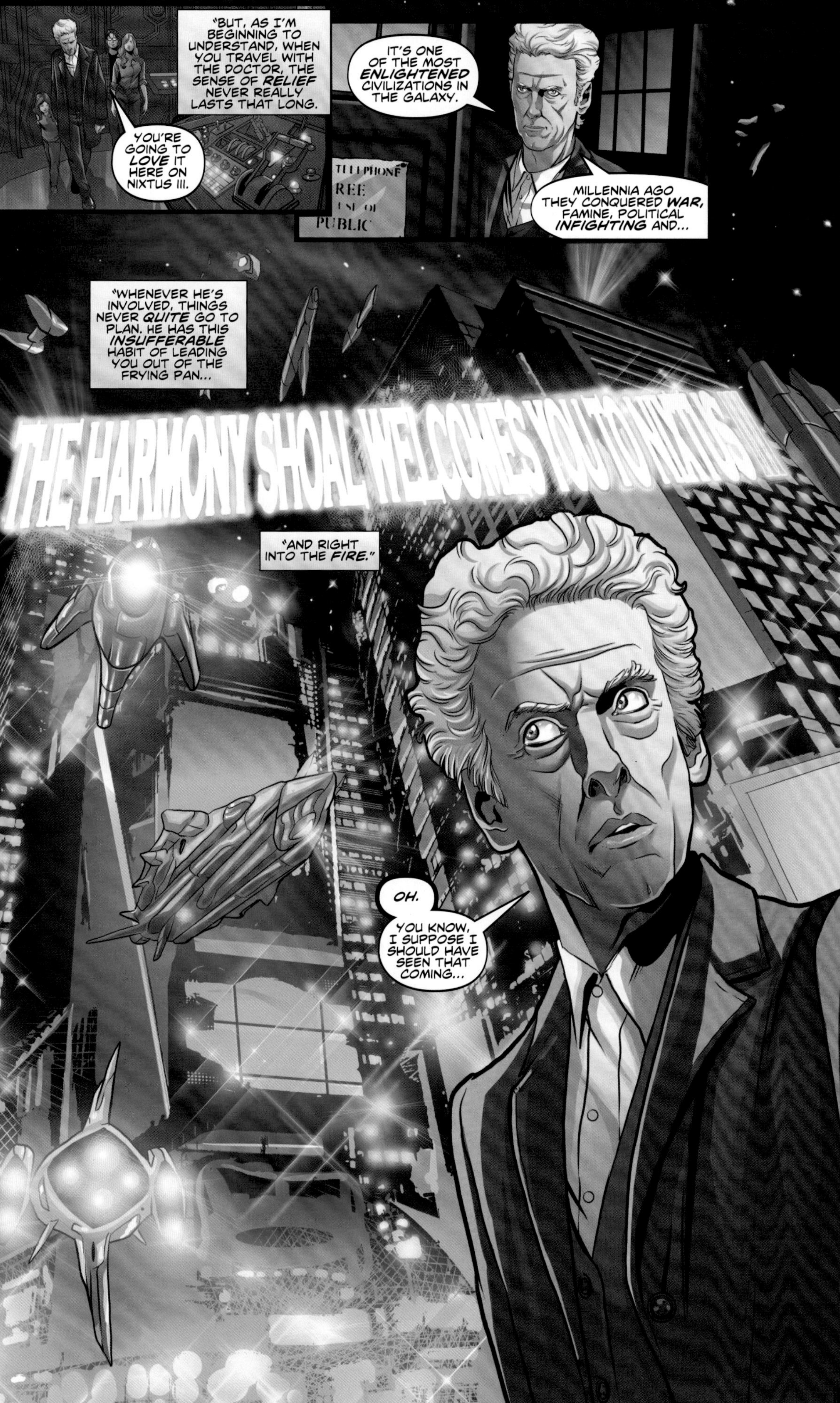
"BUT, AS I'M BEGINNING TO UNDERSTAND, WHEN YOU TRAVEL WITH THE DOCTOR, THE SENSE OF *RELIEF* NEVER REALLY LASTS THAT LONG.
YOU'RE GOING TO *LOVE* IT HERE ON NIXTUS III.
IT'S ONE OF THE MOST *ENLIGHTENED* CIVILIZATIONS IN THE GALAXY.
MILLENNIA AGO THEY CONQUERED *WAR,* FAMINE, POLITICAL *INFIGHTING* AND...
"WHENEVER HE'S INVOLVED, THINGS NEVER *QUITE* GO TO PLAN. HE HAS THIS *INSUFFERABLE* HABIT OF LEADING YOU OUT OF THE FRYING PAN...
THE HARMONY SHOAL WELCOMES YOU TO
"AND RIGHT INTO THE *FIRE.*"
OH.
YOU KNOW, I SUPPOSE I SHOULD HAVE SEEN THAT COMING...

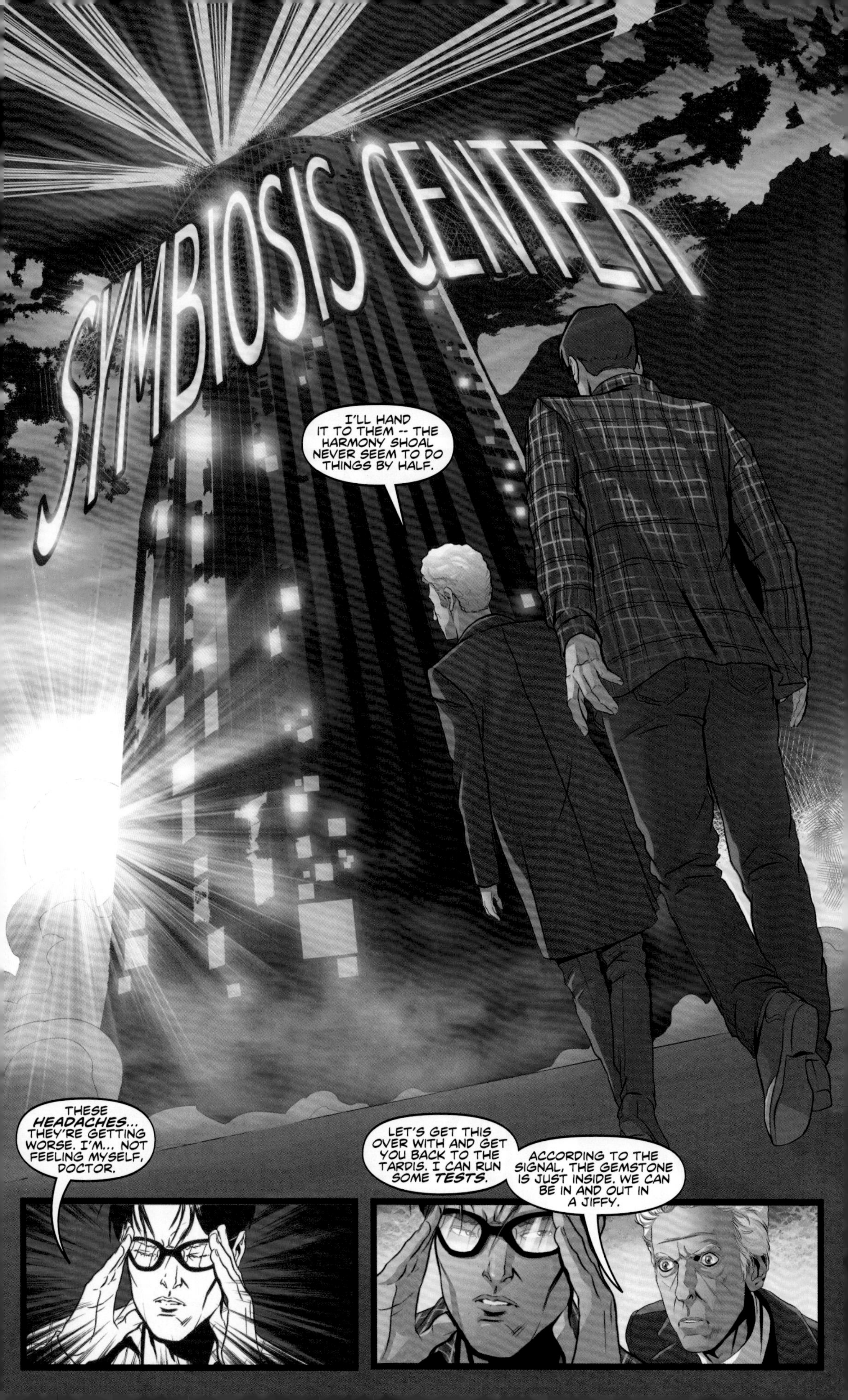
SYMBIOSIS CENTER
I'LL HAND IT TO THEM -- THE HARMONY SHOAL NEVER SEEM TO DO THINGS BY HALF.
THESE *HEADACHES*... THEY'RE GETTING WORSE. I'M... NOT FEELING MYSELF, DOCTOR.
LET'S GET THIS OVER WITH AND GET YOU BACK TO THE TARDIS. I CAN RUN SOME *TESTS*.
ACCORDING TO THE SIGNAL, THE GEMSTONE IS JUST INSIDE. WE CAN BE IN AND OUT IN A JIFFY.

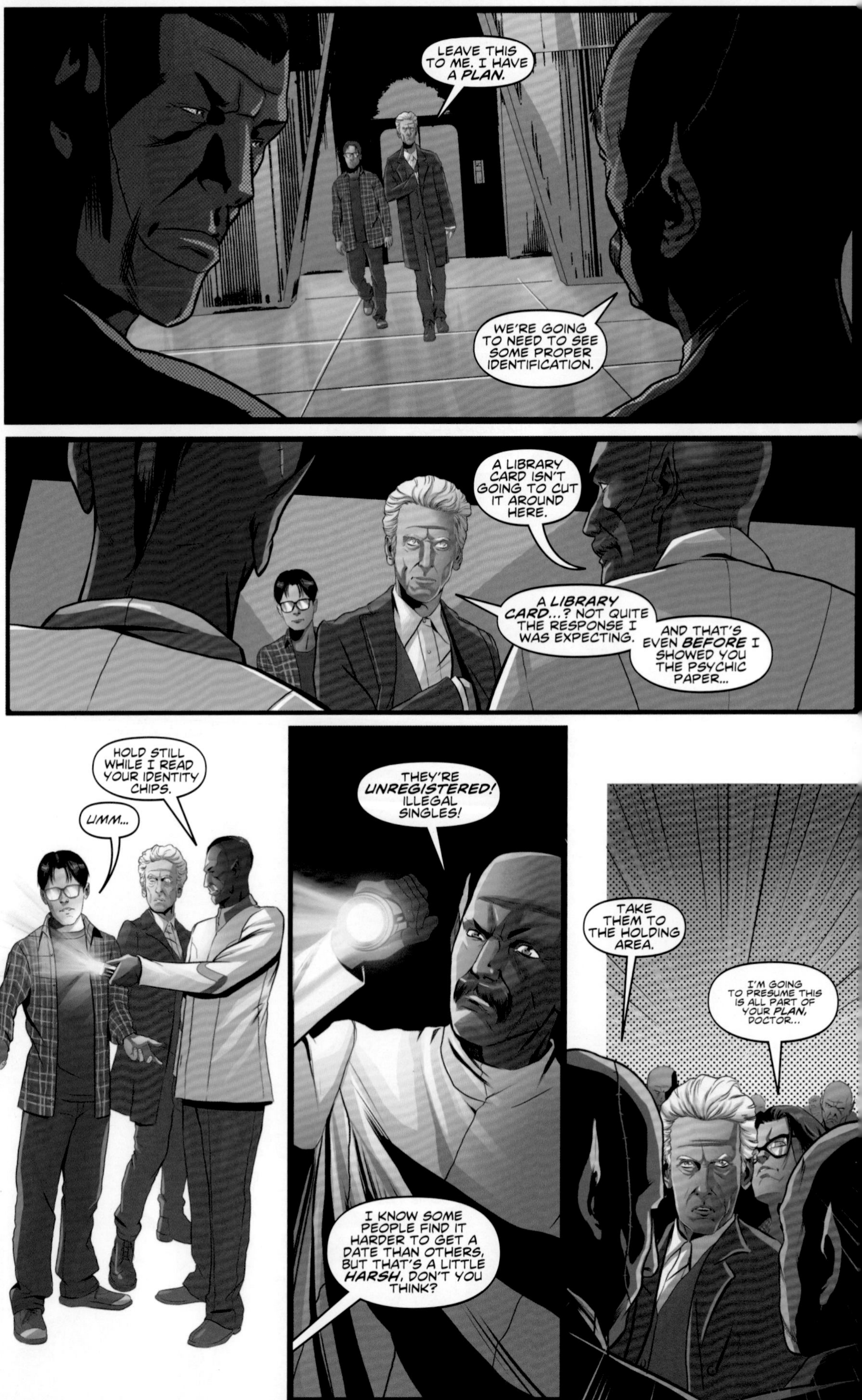
LEAVE THIS TO ME. I HAVE A *PLAN*.
WE'RE GOING TO NEED TO SEE SOME PROPER IDENTIFICATION.
A LIBRARY CARD ISN'T GOING TO CUT IT AROUND HERE.
A *LIBRARY CARD*...? NOT QUITE THE RESPONSE I WAS EXPECTING.
AND THAT'S EVEN *BEFORE* I SHOWED YOU THE PSYCHIC PAPER...
HOLD STILL WHILE I READ YOUR IDENTITY CHIPS.
UMM...
THEY'RE *UNREGISTERED!* ILLEGAL SINGLES!
I KNOW SOME PEOPLE FIND IT HARDER TO GET A DATE THAN OTHERS, BUT THAT'S A LITTLE *HARSH*, DON'T YOU THINK?
TAKE THEM TO THE HOLDING AREA.
I'M GOING TO PRESUME THIS IS ALL PART OF YOUR *PLAN*, DOCTOR...

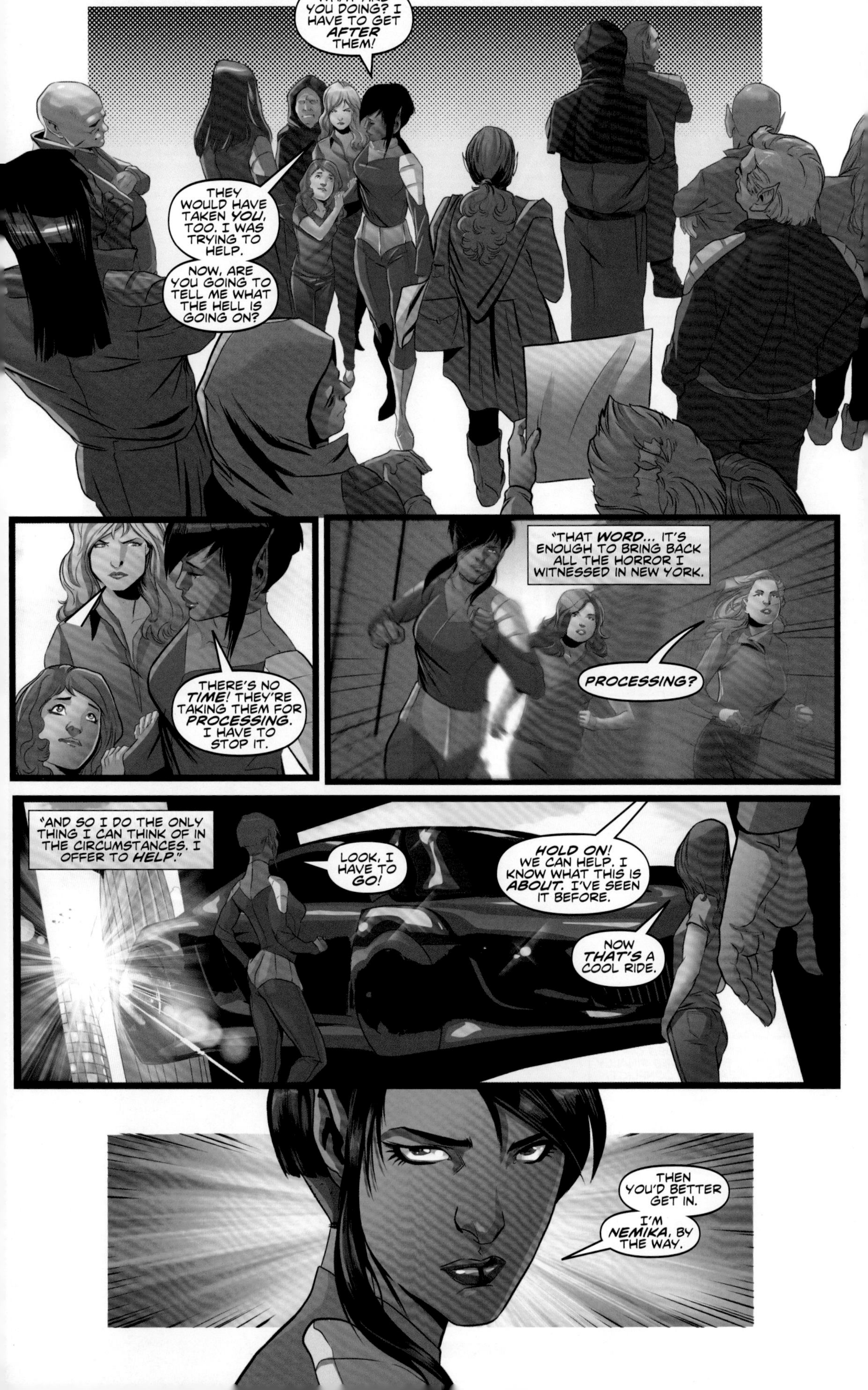
WHAT ARE YOU DOING? I HAVE TO GET *AFTER* THEM!
THEY WOULD HAVE TAKEN *YOU*, TOO. I WAS TRYING TO HELP.
NOW, ARE YOU GOING TO TELL ME WHAT THE HELL IS GOING ON?
THERE'S NO *TIME*! THEY'RE TAKING THEM FOR *PROCESSING*. I HAVE TO STOP IT.
"THAT *WORD*... IT'S ENOUGH TO BRING BACK ALL THE HORROR I WITNESSED IN NEW YORK.
PROCESSING?
"AND SO I DO THE ONLY THING I CAN THINK OF IN THE CIRCUMSTANCES. I OFFER TO *HELP*."
LOOK, I HAVE TO *GO*!
HOLD ON! WE CAN HELP. I KNOW WHAT THIS IS *ABOUT*. I'VE SEEN IT BEFORE.
NOW *THAT'S* A COOL RIDE.
THEN YOU'D BETTER GET IN.
I'M *NEMIKA*, BY THE WAY.

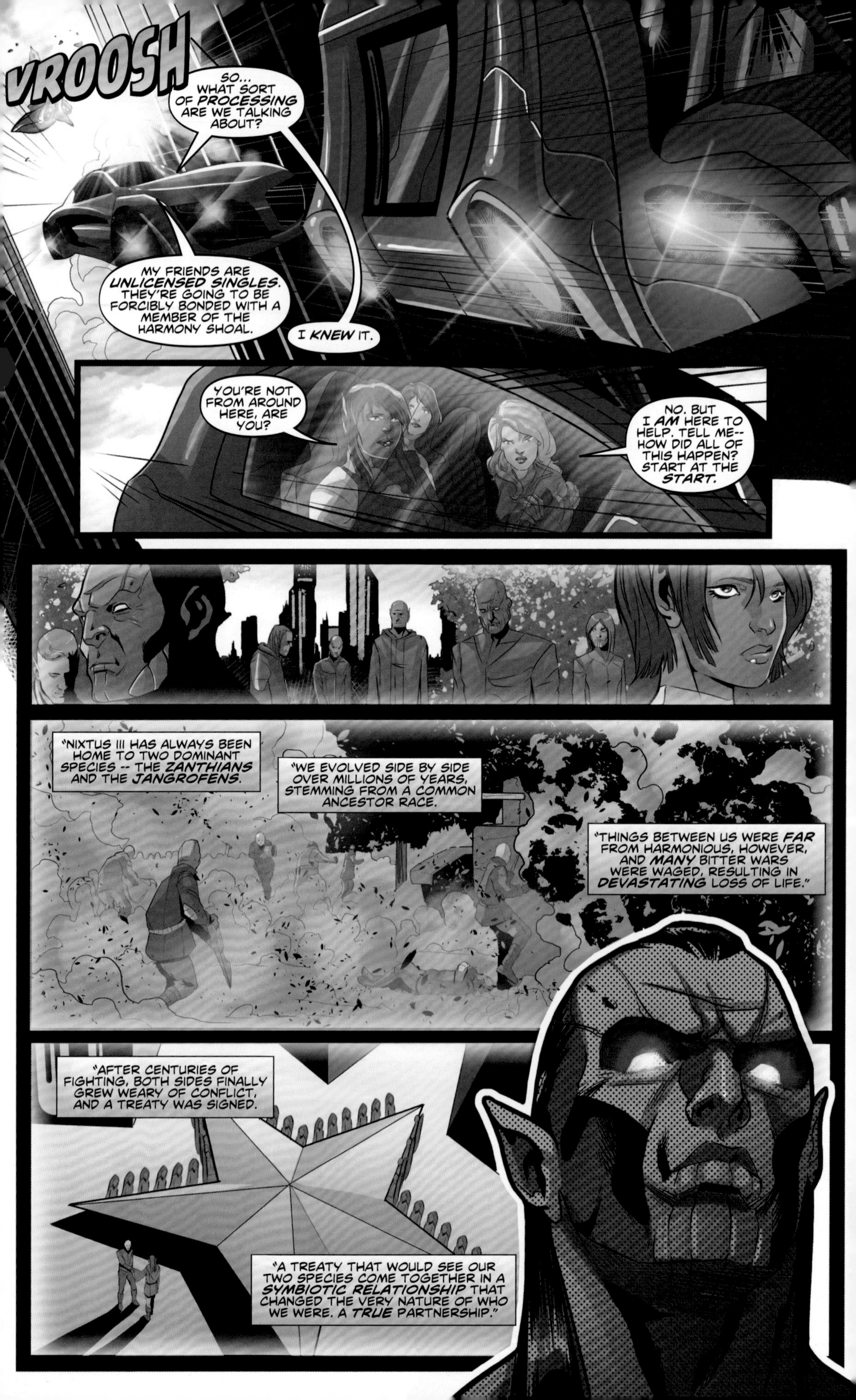
VROOSH
SO... WHAT SORT OF PROCESSING ARE WE TALKING ABOUT?
MY FRIENDS ARE UNLICENSED SINGLES. THEY'RE GOING TO BE FORCIBLY BONDED WITH A MEMBER OF THE HARMONY SHOAL.
I KNEW IT.
YOU'RE NOT FROM AROUND HERE, ARE YOU?
NO. BUT I AM HERE TO HELP. TELL ME-- HOW DID ALL OF THIS HAPPEN? START AT THE START.
"NIXTUS III HAS ALWAYS BEEN HOME TO TWO DOMINANT SPECIES -- THE ZANTHIANS AND THE JANGROFENS.
"WE EVOLVED SIDE BY SIDE OVER MILLIONS OF YEARS, STEMMING FROM A COMMON ANCESTOR RACE.
"THINGS BETWEEN US WERE FAR FROM HARMONIOUS, HOWEVER, AND MANY BITTER WARS WERE WAGED, RESULTING IN DEVASTATING LOSS OF LIFE."
"AFTER CENTURIES OF FIGHTING, BOTH SIDES FINALLY GREW WEARY OF CONFLICT, AND A TREATY WAS SIGNED.
"A TREATY THAT WOULD SEE OUR TWO SPECIES COME TOGETHER IN A SYMBIOTIC RELATIONSHIP THAT CHANGED THE VERY NATURE OF WHO WE WERE. A TRUE PARTNERSHIP."

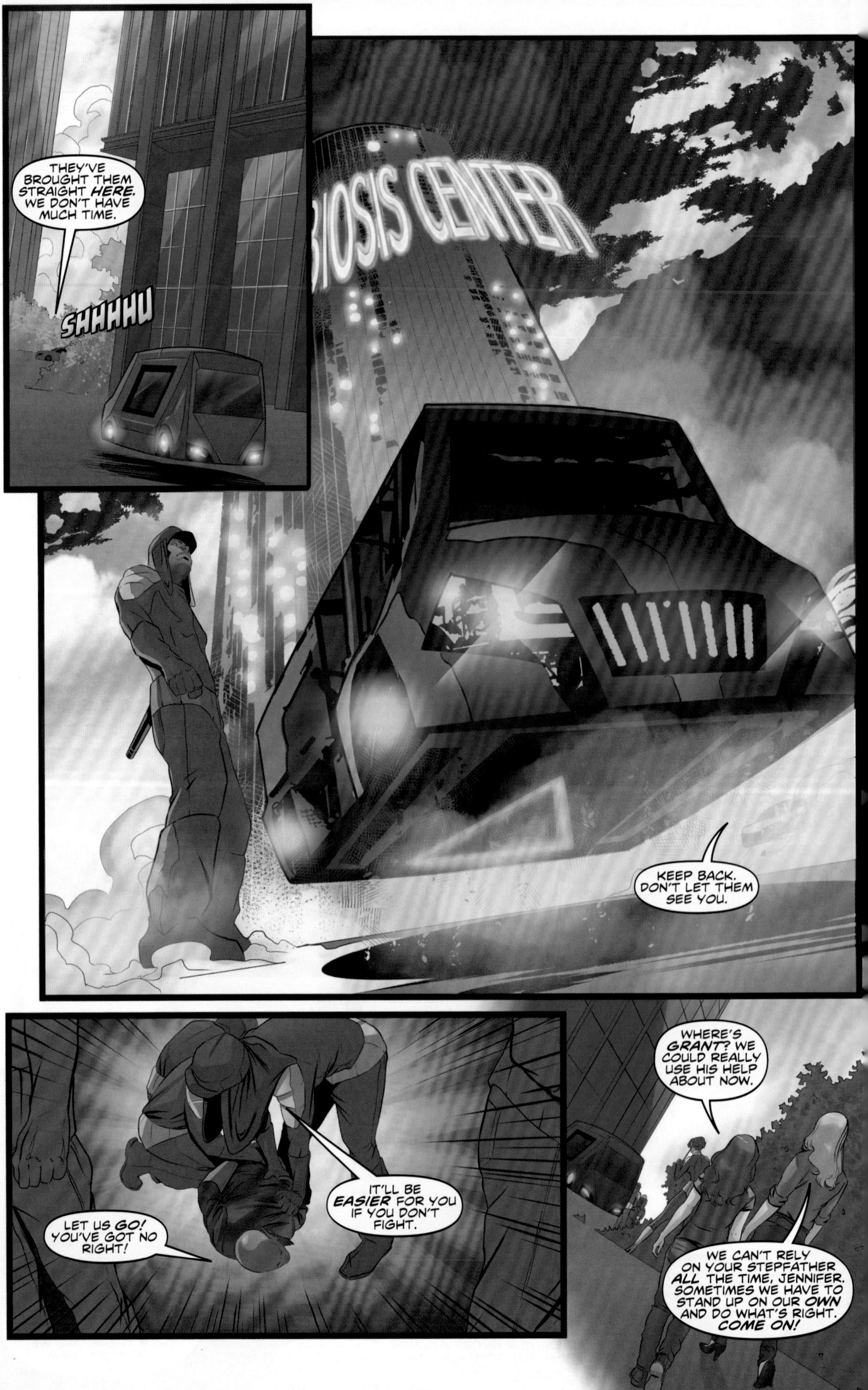
THEY'VE BROUGHT THEM STRAIGHT HERE. WE DON'T HAVE MUCH TIME.
SHHHHU
BIOSIS CENTER
KEEP BACK. DON'T LET THEM SEE YOU.
LET US GO! YOU'VE GOT NO RIGHT!
IT'LL BE EASIER FOR YOU IF YOU DON'T FIGHT.
WHERE'S GRANT? WE COULD REALLY USE HIS HELP ABOUT NOW.
WE CAN'T RELY ON YOUR STEPFATHER ALL THE TIME, JENNIFER. SOMETIMES WE HAVE TO STAND UP ON OUR OWN AND DO WHAT'S RIGHT. COME ON!

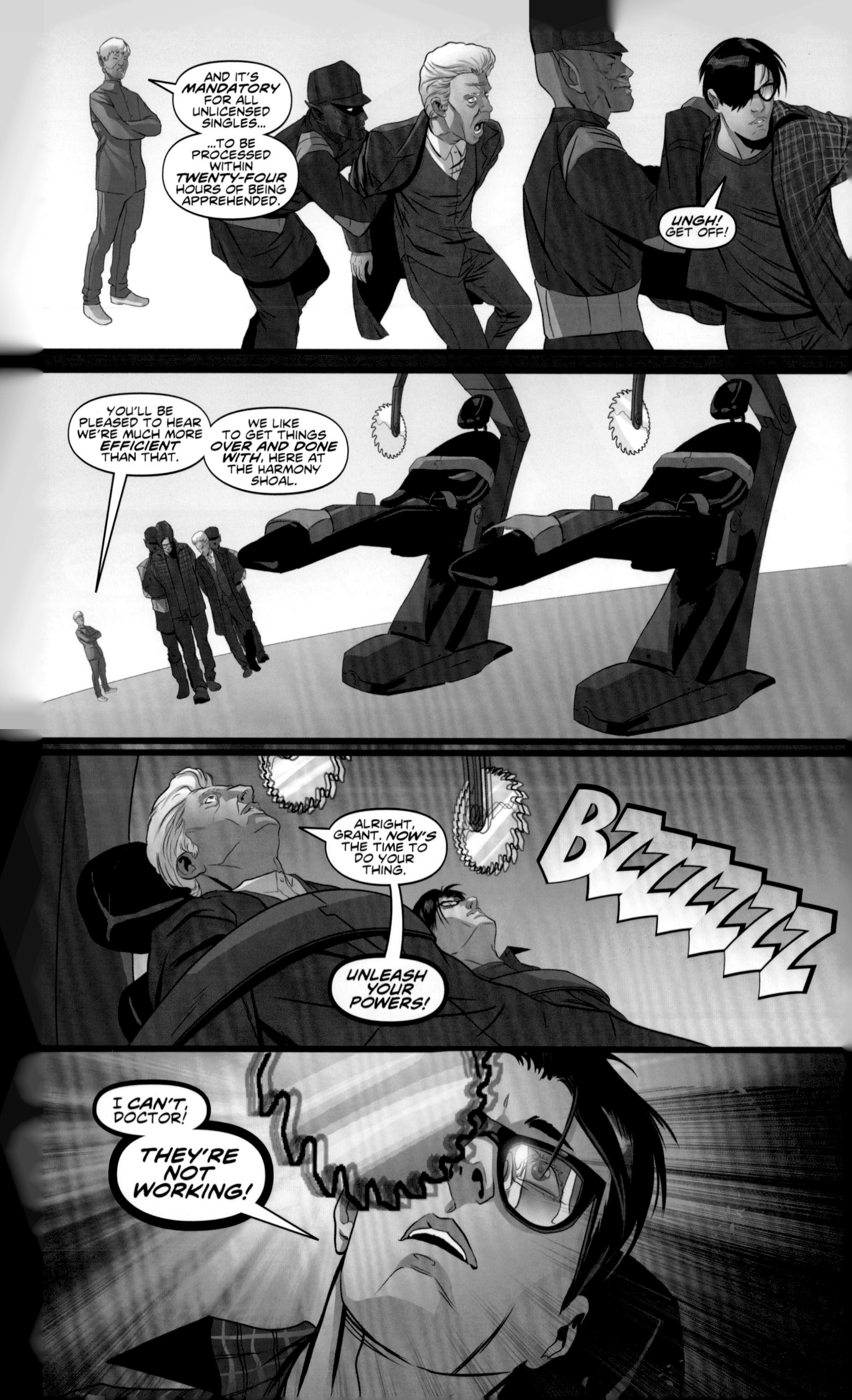

AND IT'S MANDATORY FOR ALL UNLICENSED SINGLES...
...TO BE PROCESSED WITHIN TWENTY-FOUR HOURS OF BEING APPREHENDED.
UNGH! GET OFF!
YOU'LL BE PLEASED TO HEAR WE'RE MUCH MORE EFFICIENT THAN THAT.
WE LIKE TO GET THINGS OVER AND DONE WITH, HERE AT THE HARMONY SHOAL.
ALRIGHT, GRANT. NOW'S THE TIME TO DO YOUR THING.
UNLEASH YOUR POWERS!
BZZZZZ
I CAN'T, DOCTOR!
THEY'RE NOT WORKING!

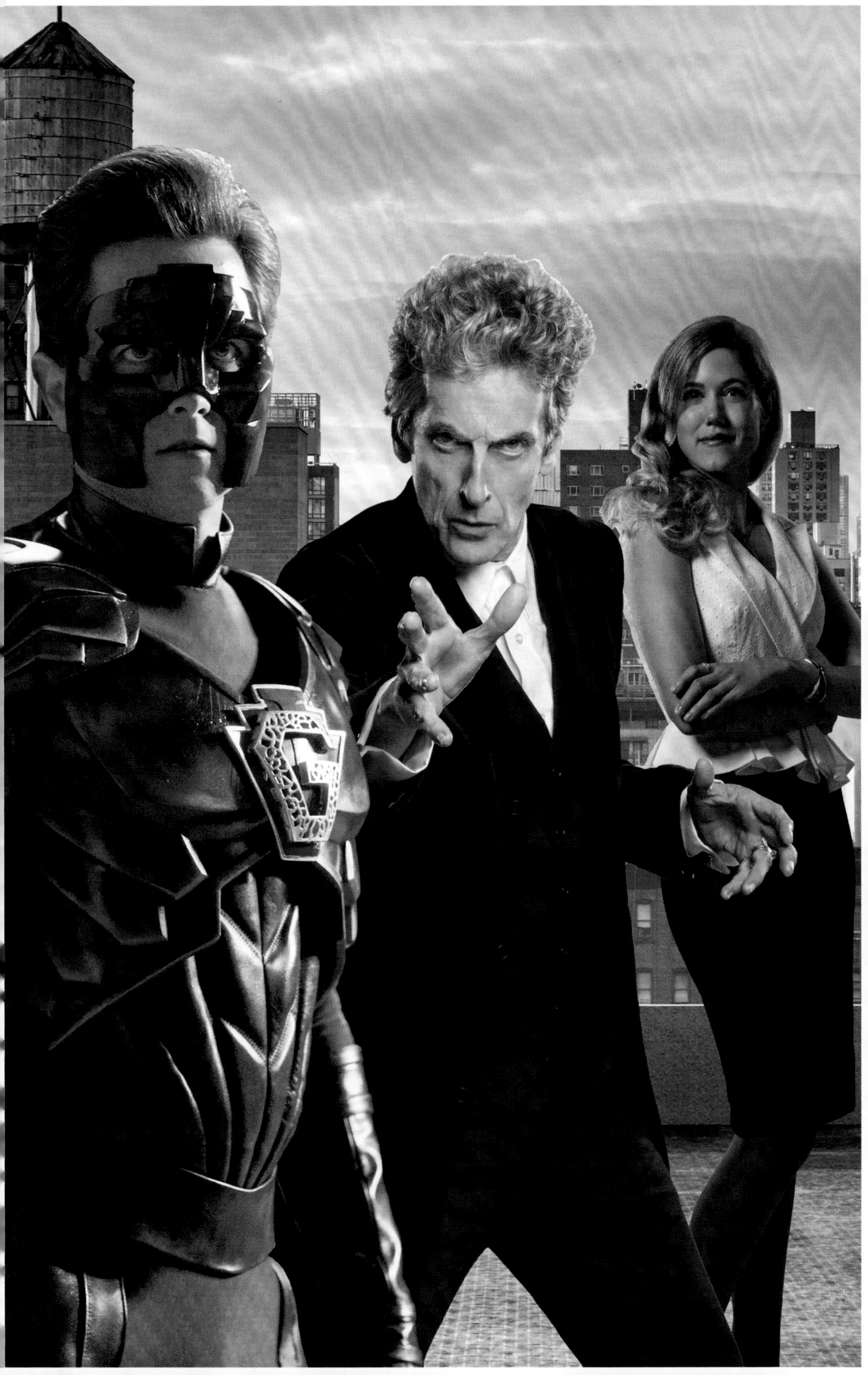

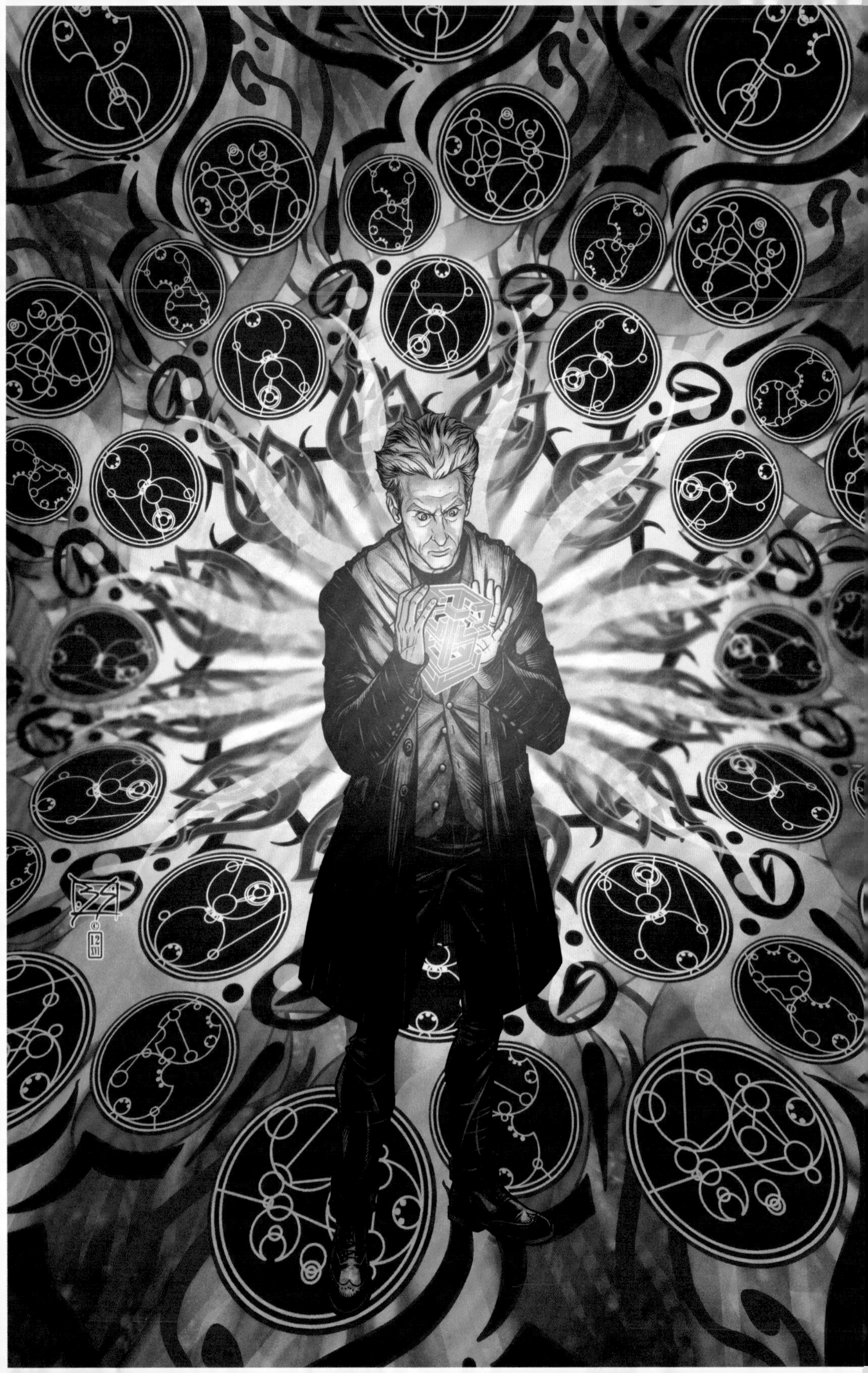

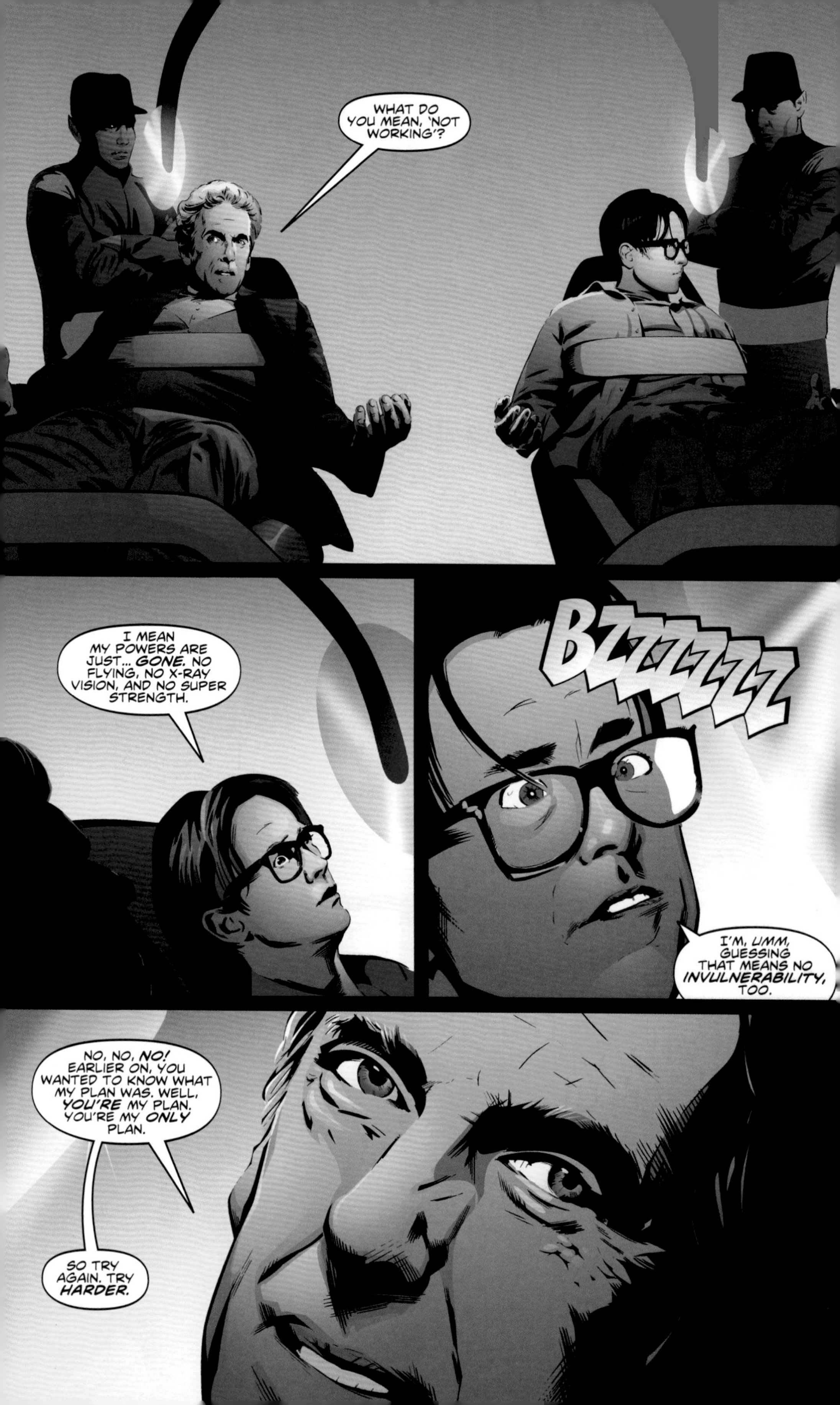
WHAT DO YOU MEAN, 'NOT WORKING'?
I MEAN MY POWERS ARE JUST... **GONE.** NO FLYING, NO X-RAY VISION, AND NO SUPER STRENGTH.
BZZZZZZ
I'M, *UMM,* GUESSING THAT MEANS NO ***INVULNERABILITY,*** TOO.
NO, NO, ***NO!*** EARLIER ON, YOU WANTED TO KNOW WHAT MY PLAN WAS. WELL, ***YOU'RE*** MY PLAN. YOU'RE MY ***ONLY*** PLAN.
SO TRY AGAIN. TRY ***HARDER.***

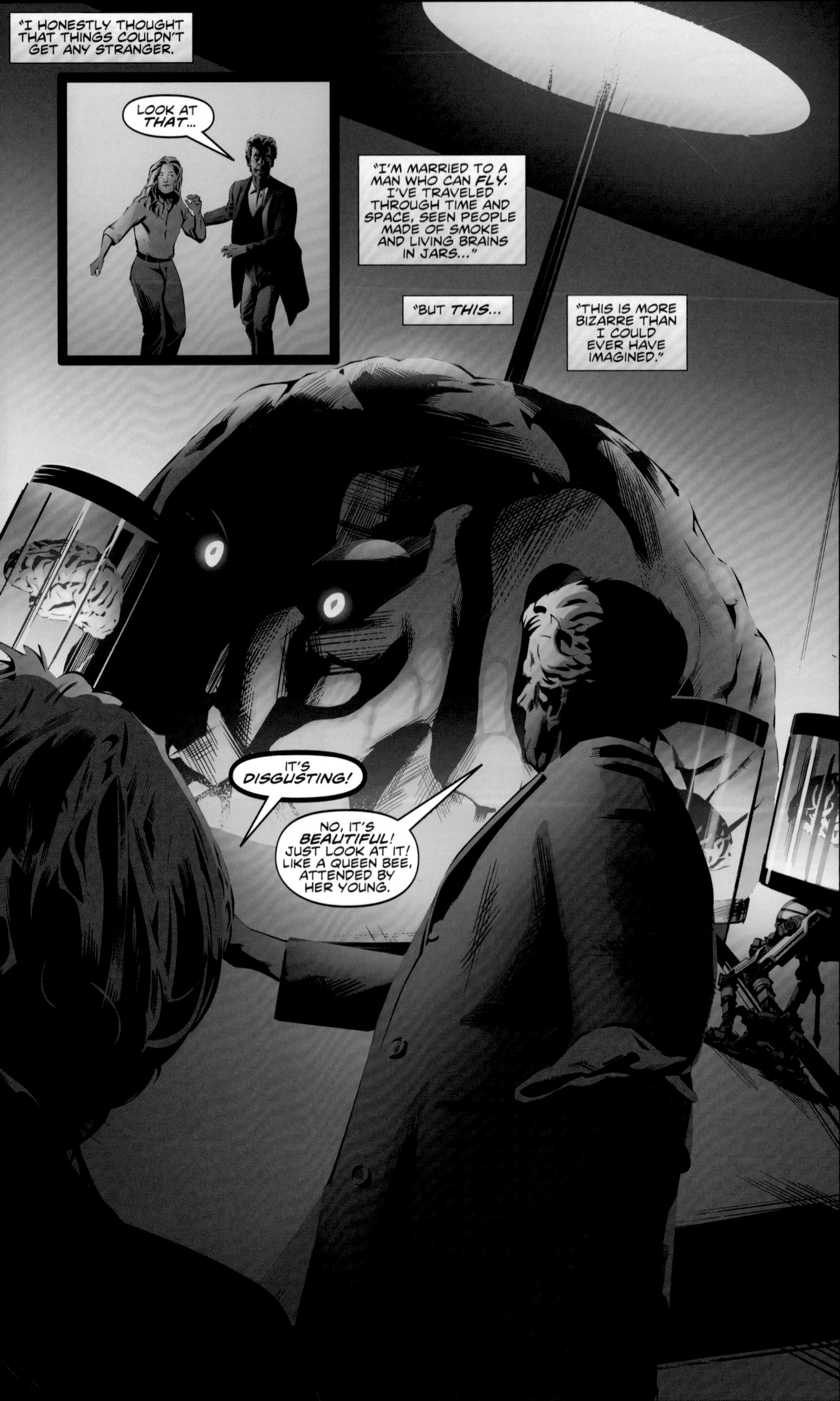
"I HONESTLY THOUGHT THAT THINGS COULDN'T GET ANY STRANGER.
LOOK AT *THAT*...
"I'M MARRIED TO A MAN WHO CAN *FLY*. I'VE TRAVELED THROUGH TIME AND SPACE, SEEN PEOPLE MADE OF SMOKE AND LIVING BRAINS IN JARS..."
"BUT *THIS*...
"THIS IS MORE BIZARRE THAN I COULD EVER HAVE IMAGINED."
IT'S *DISGUSTING!*
NO, IT'S *BEAUTIFUL!* JUST LOOK AT IT! LIKE A QUEEN BEE, ATTENDED BY HER YOUNG.

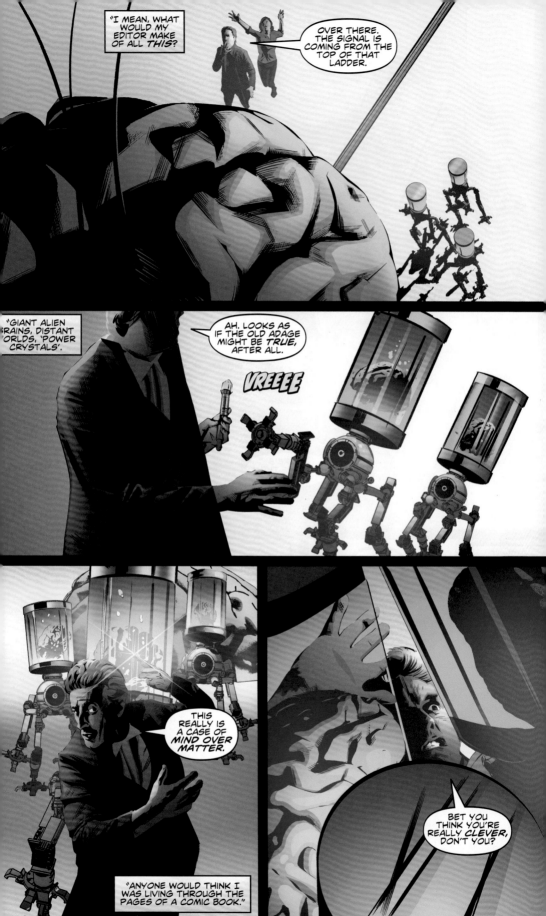

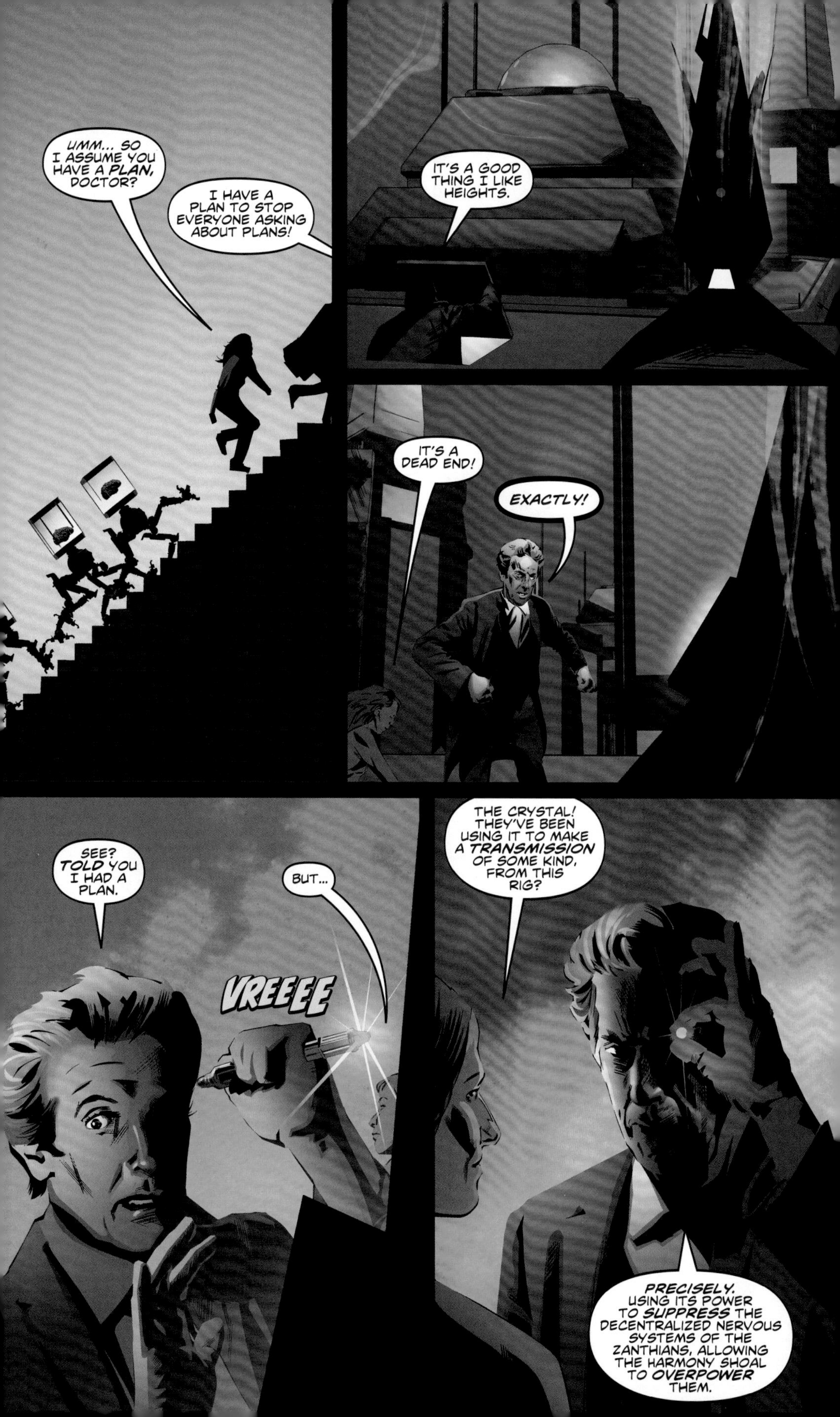
UMM... SO I ASSUME YOU HAVE A PLAN, DOCTOR?
I HAVE A PLAN TO STOP EVERYONE ASKING ABOUT PLANS!
IT'S A GOOD THING I LIKE HEIGHTS.
IT'S A DEAD END!
EXACTLY!
SEE? TOLD YOU I HAD A PLAN.
BUT...
VREEEE
THE CRYSTAL! THEY'VE BEEN USING IT TO MAKE A TRANSMISSION OF SOME KIND, FROM THIS RIG?
PRECISELY. USING ITS POWER TO SUPPRESS THE DECENTRALIZED NERVOUS SYSTEMS OF THE ZANTHIANS, ALLOWING THE HARMONY SHOAL TO OVERPOWER THEM.

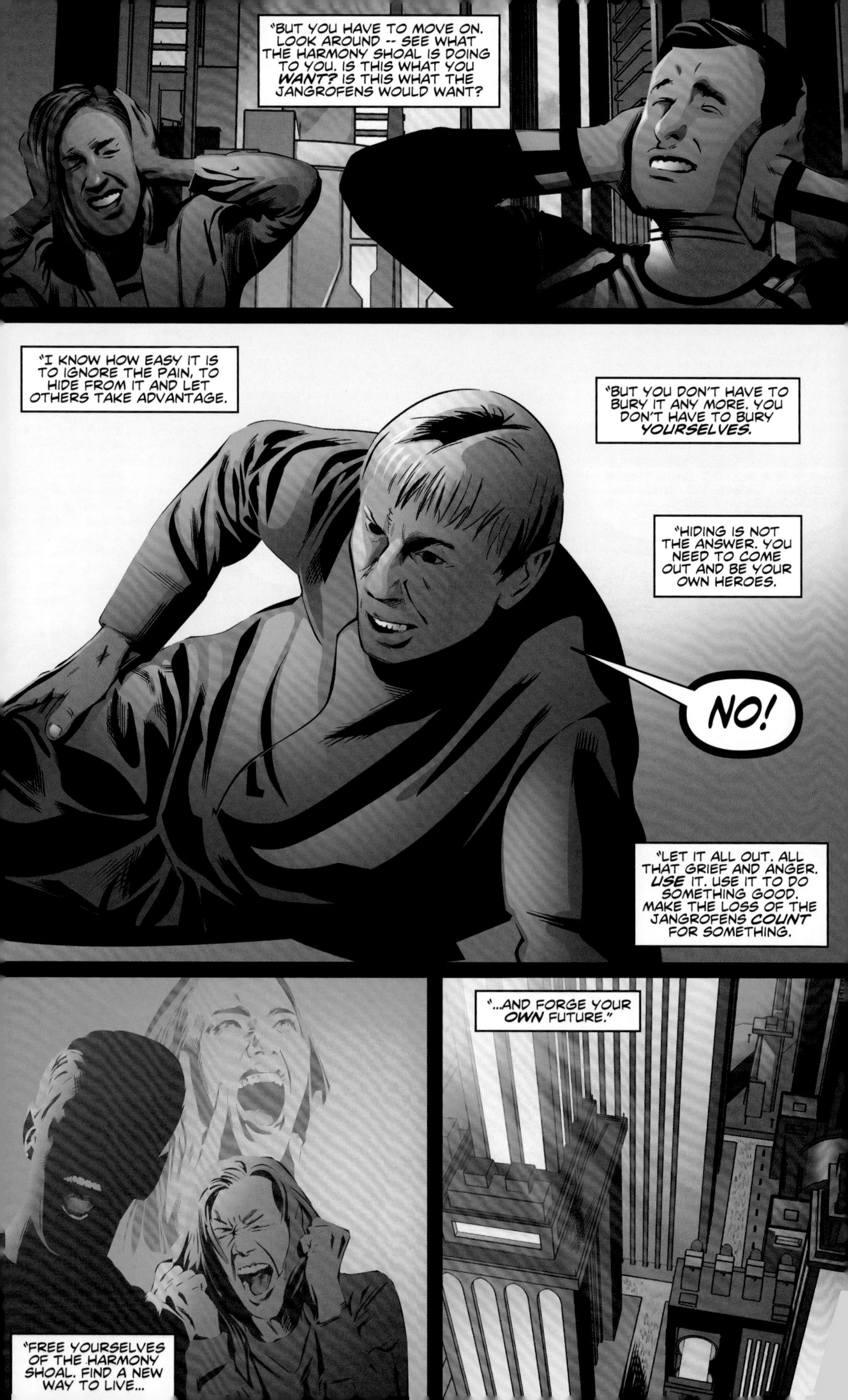
"BUT YOU HAVE TO MOVE ON. LOOK AROUND -- SEE WHAT THE HARMONY SHOAL IS DOING TO YOU. IS THIS WHAT YOU *WANT?* IS THIS WHAT THE JANGROFENS WOULD WANT?
"I KNOW HOW EASY IT IS TO IGNORE THE PAIN, TO HIDE FROM IT AND LET OTHERS TAKE ADVANTAGE.
"BUT YOU DON'T HAVE TO BURY IT ANY MORE. YOU DON'T HAVE TO BURY *YOURSELVES.*
"HIDING IS NOT THE ANSWER. YOU NEED TO COME OUT AND BE YOUR OWN HEROES.
NO!
"LET IT ALL OUT. ALL THAT GRIEF AND ANGER. *USE* IT. USE IT TO DO SOMETHING GOOD. MAKE THE LOSS OF THE JANGROFENS *COUNT* FOR SOMETHING.
"FREE YOURSELVES OF THE HARMONY SHOAL. FIND A NEW WAY TO LIVE...
"...AND FORGE YOUR *OWN* FUTURE."

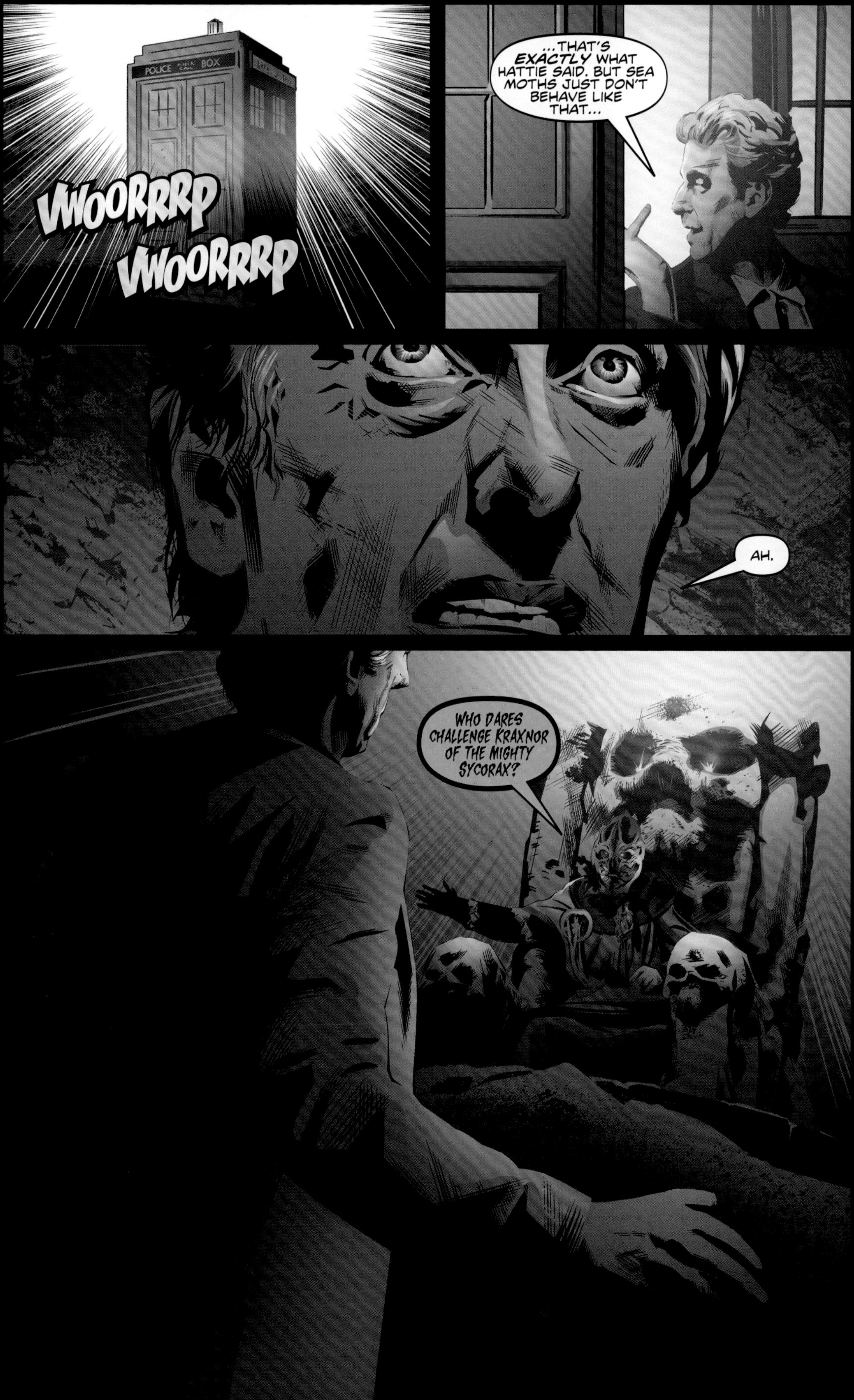
POLICE PUBLIC CALL BOX
VWOORRRP
VWOORRRP
...THAT'S EXACTLY WHAT HATTIE SAID. BUT SEA MOTHS JUST DON'T BEHAVE LIKE THAT...
AH.
WHO DARES CHALLENGE KRAXNOR OF THE MIGHTY SYCORAX?

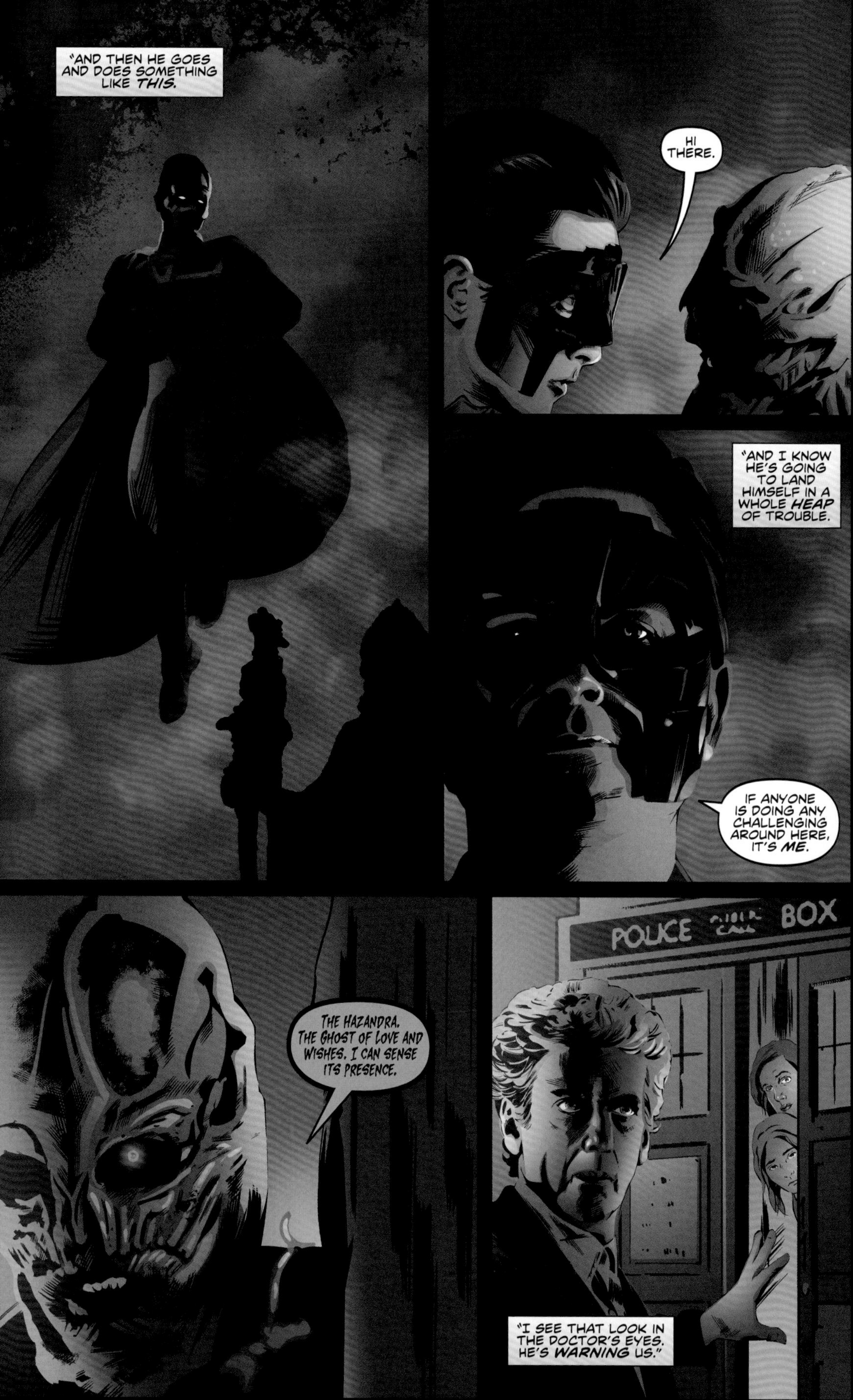

"AND THEN HE GOES AND DOES SOMETHING LIKE THIS.
HI THERE.
"AND I KNOW HE'S GOING TO LAND HIMSELF IN A WHOLE HEAP OF TROUBLE.
IF ANYONE IS DOING ANY CHALLENGING AROUND HERE, IT'S ME.
THE HAZANDRA. THE GHOST OF LOVE AND WISHES. I CAN SENSE ITS PRESENCE.
POLICE BOX
"I SEE THAT LOOK IN THE DOCTOR'S EYES. HE'S WARNING US."

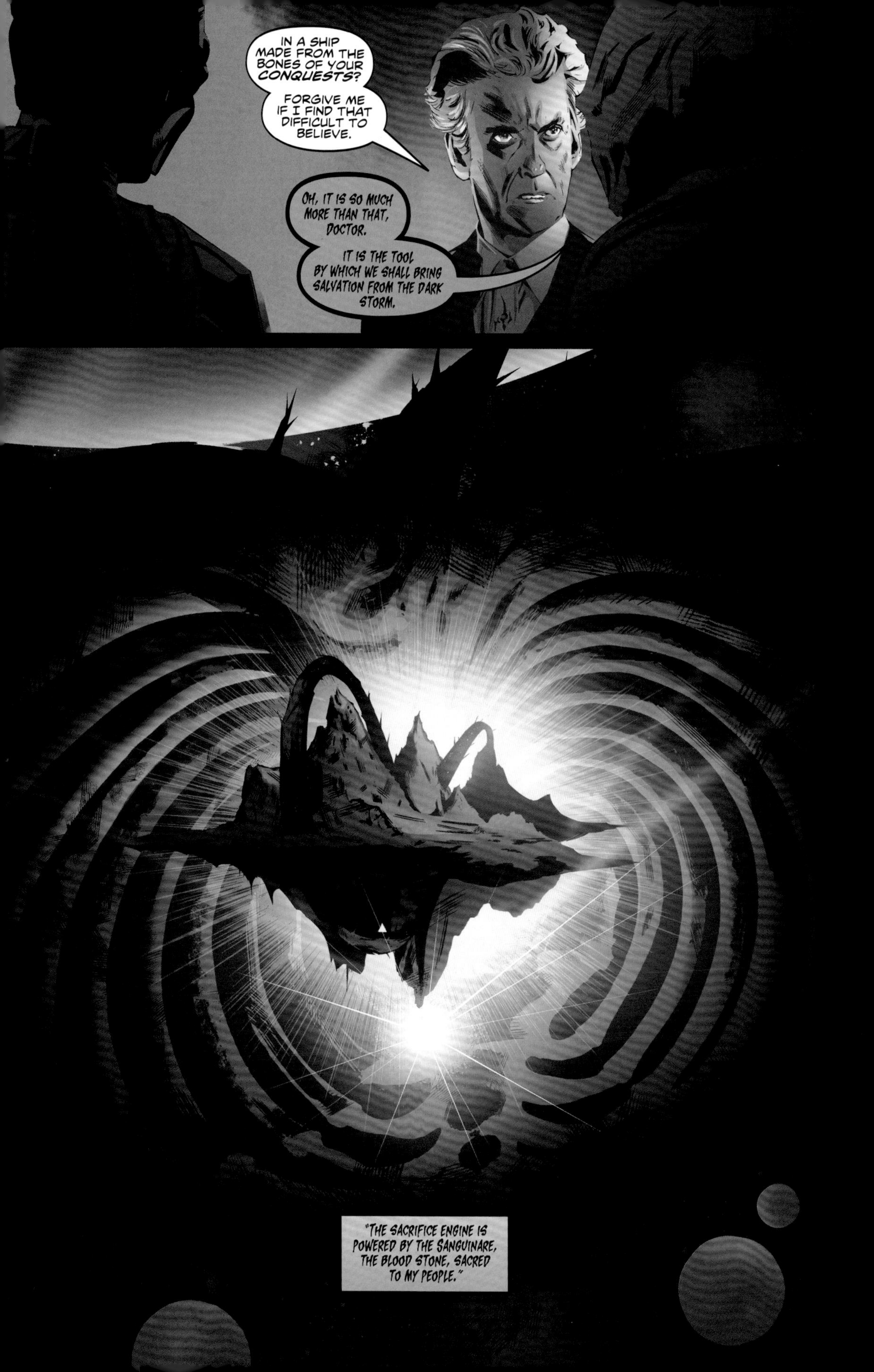

IN A SHIP MADE FROM THE BONES OF YOUR CONQUESTS?
FORGIVE ME IF I FIND THAT DIFFICULT TO BELIEVE.
OH, IT IS SO MUCH MORE THAN THAT, DOCTOR.
IT IS THE TOOL BY WHICH WE SHALL BRING SALVATION FROM THE DARK STORM.
"THE SACRIFICE ENGINE IS POWERED BY THE SANGUINARE, THE BLOOD STONE, SACRED TO MY PEOPLE."

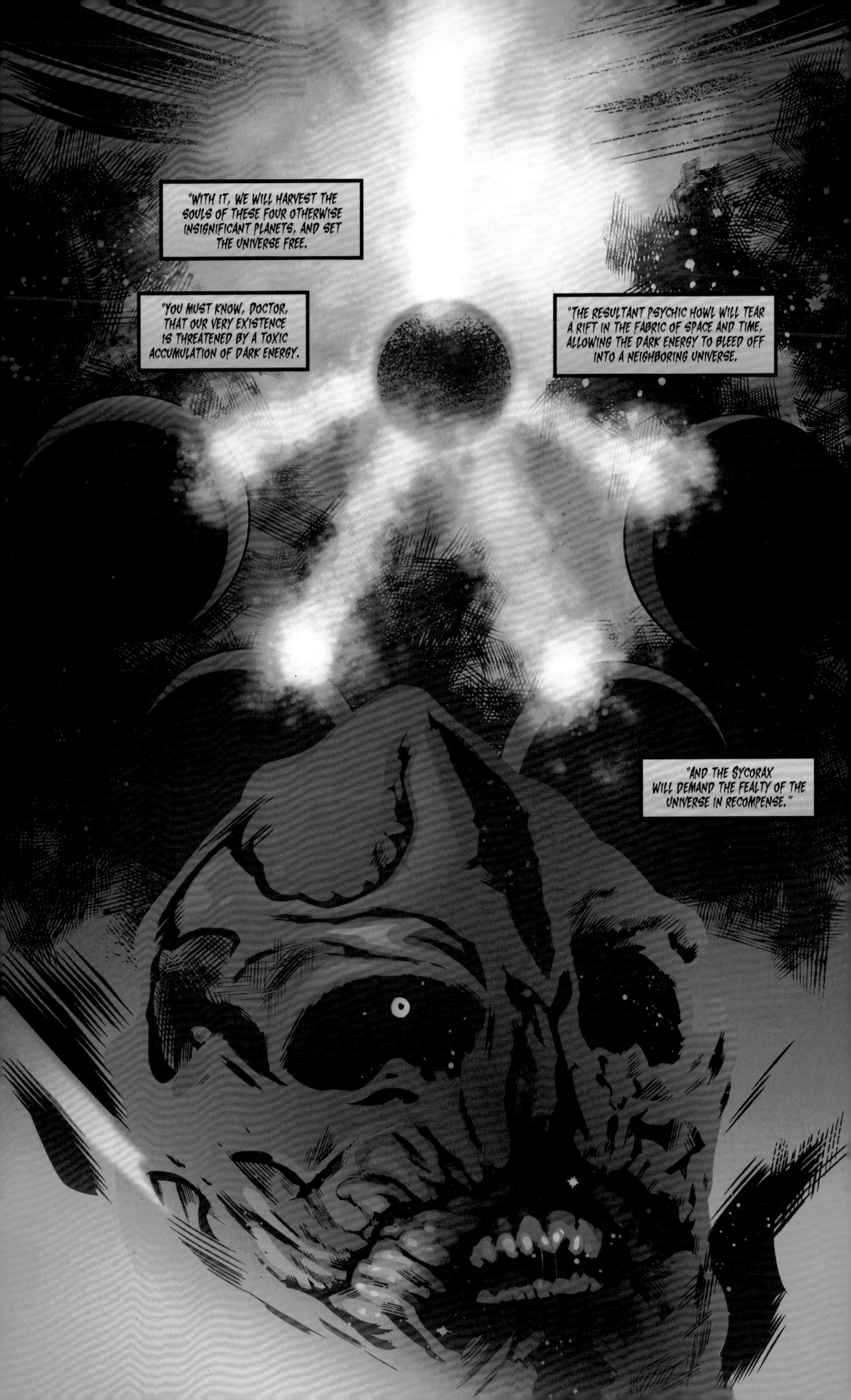
"WITH IT, WE WILL HARVEST THE SOULS OF THESE FOUR OTHERWISE INSIGNIFICANT PLANETS, AND SET THE UNIVERSE FREE.
"YOU MUST KNOW, DOCTOR, THAT OUR VERY EXISTENCE IS THREATENED BY A TOXIC ACCUMULATION OF DARK ENERGY.
"THE RESULTANT PSYCHIC HOWL WILL TEAR A RIFT IN THE FABRIC OF SPACE AND TIME, ALLOWING THE DARK ENERGY TO BLEED OFF INTO A NEIGHBORING UNIVERSE.
"AND THE SYCORAX WILL DEMAND THE FEALTY OF THE UNIVERSE IN RECOMPENSE."

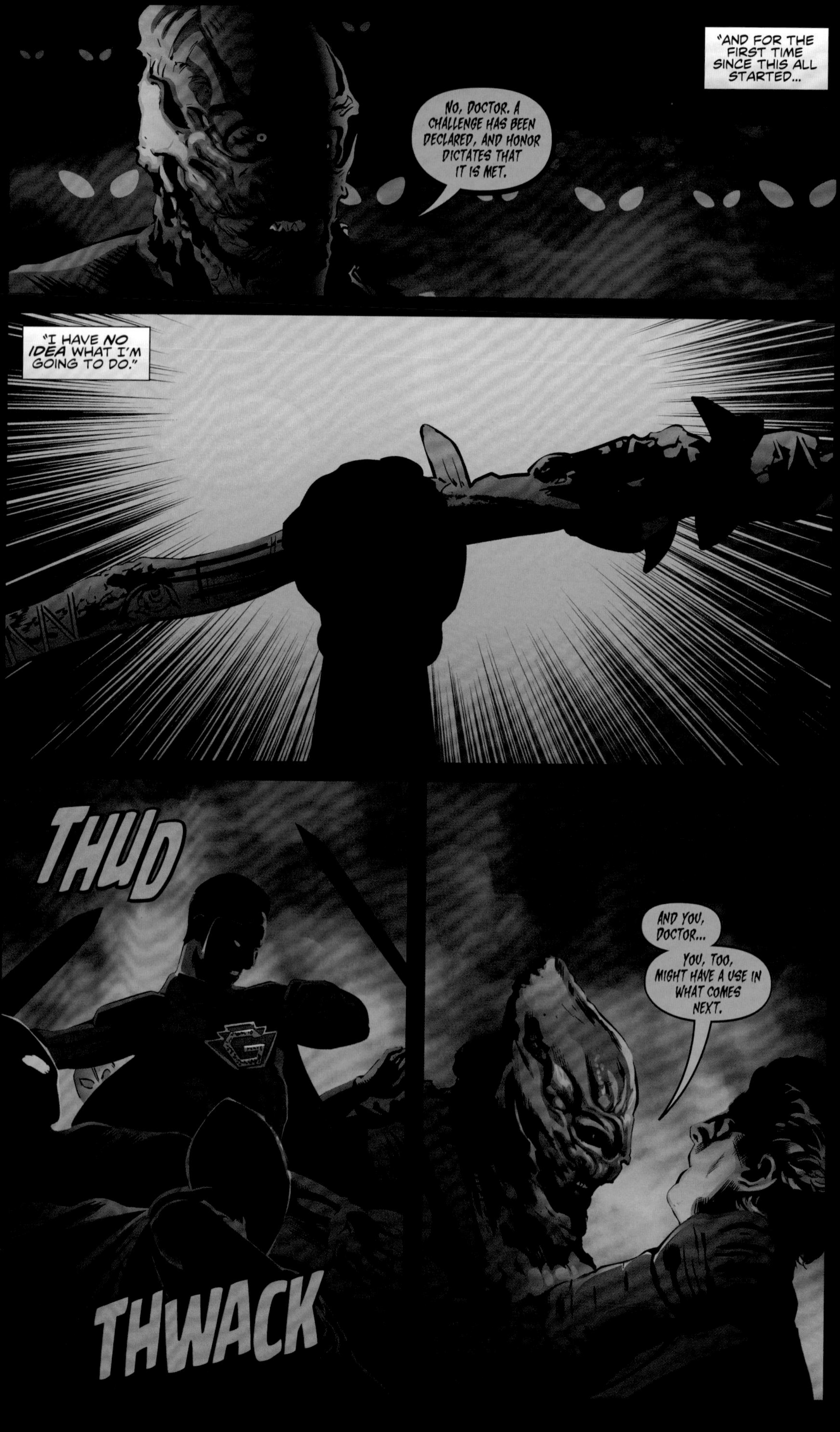
"AND FOR THE FIRST TIME SINCE THIS ALL STARTED...
NO, DOCTOR. A CHALLENGE HAS BEEN DECLARED, AND HONOR DICTATES THAT IT IS MET.
"I HAVE NO IDEA WHAT I'M GOING TO DO."
THUD
THWACK
AND YOU, DOCTOR...
YOU, TOO, MIGHT HAVE A USE IN WHAT COMES NEXT.

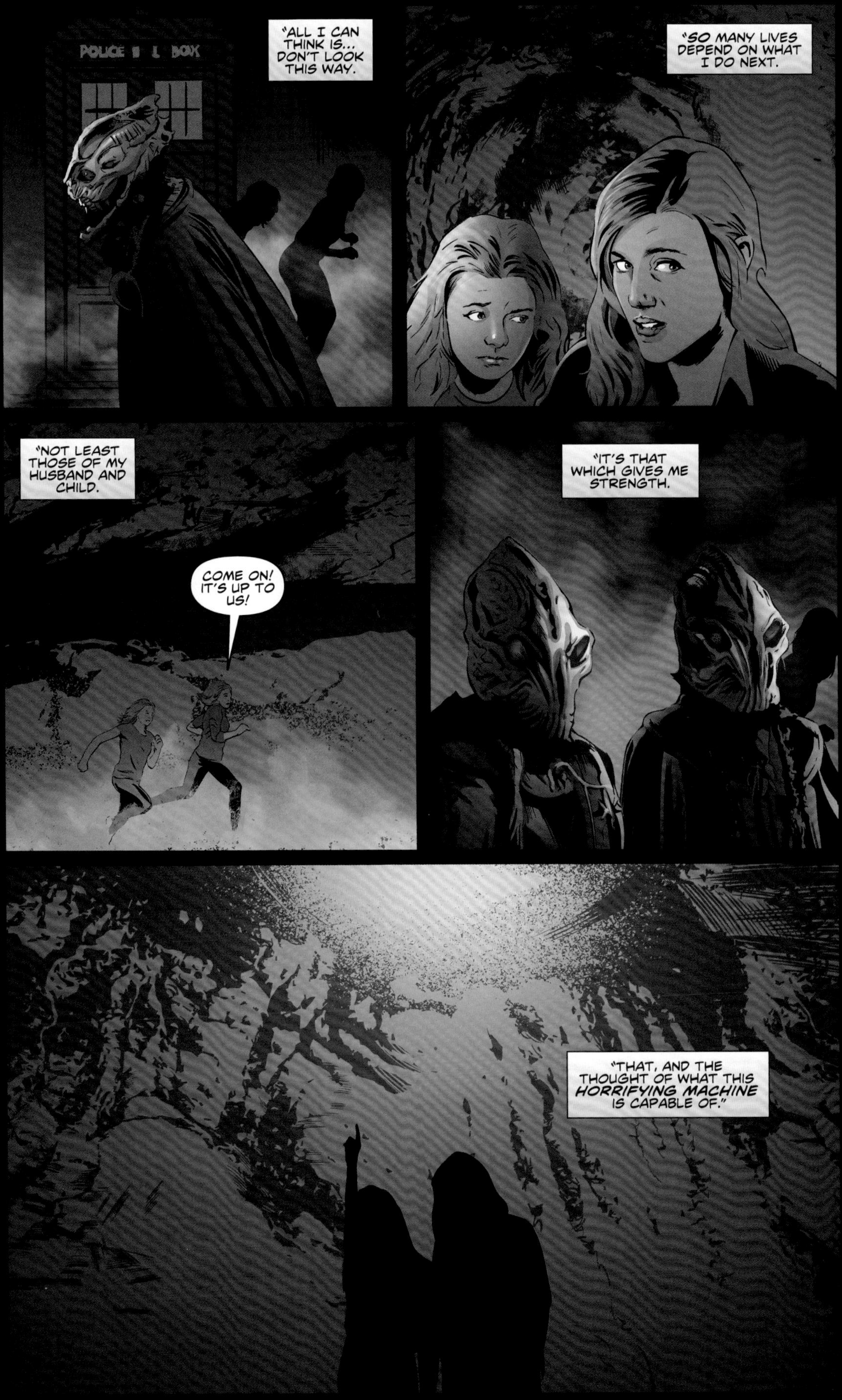
POLICE BOX
"ALL I CAN THINK IS... DON'T LOOK THIS WAY.
"SO MANY LIVES DEPEND ON WHAT I DO NEXT.
"NOT LEAST THOSE OF MY HUSBAND AND CHILD.
COME ON! IT'S UP TO US!
"IT'S THAT WHICH GIVES ME STRENGTH.
"THAT, AND THE THOUGHT OF WHAT THIS *HORRIFYING MACHINE* IS CAPABLE OF."

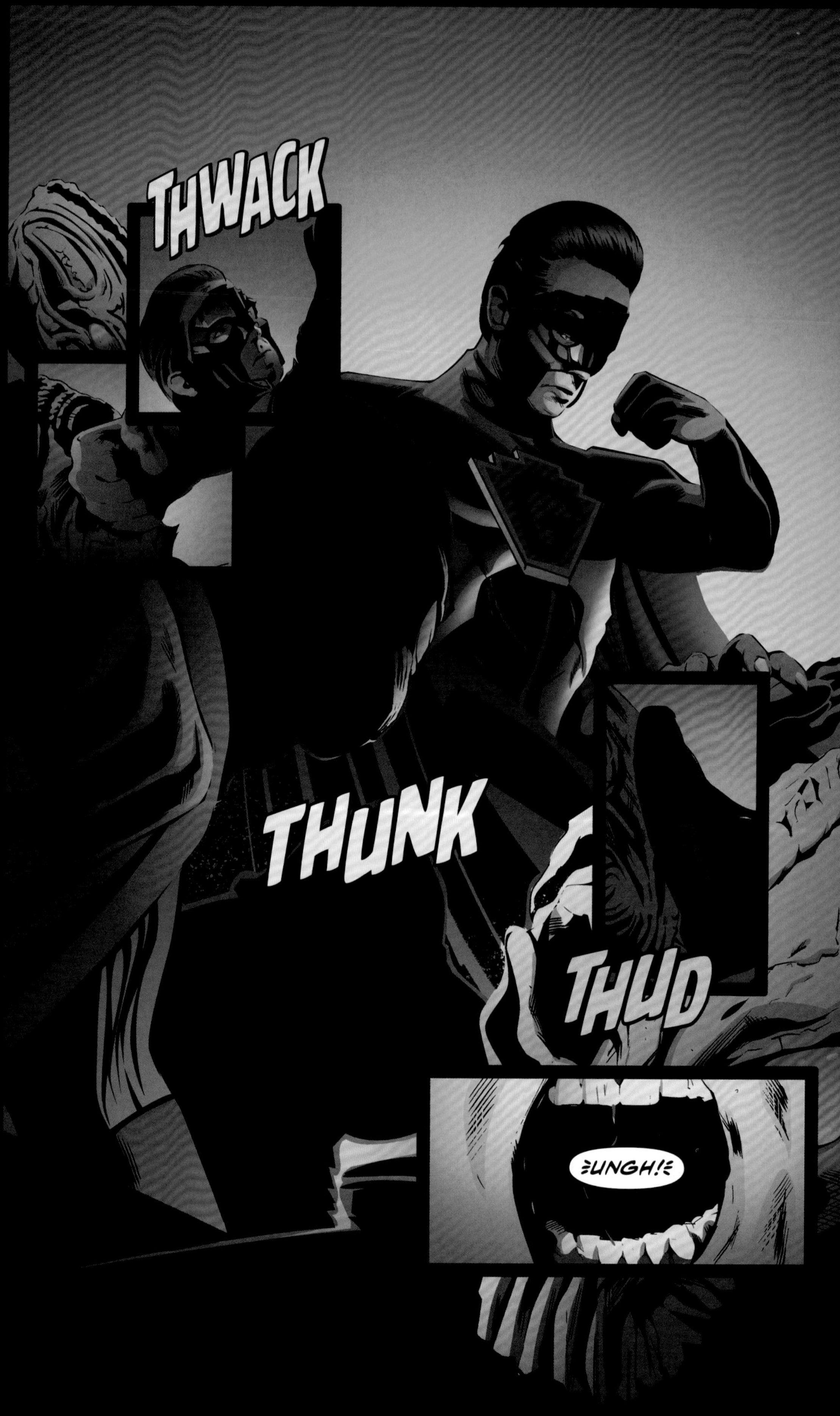
THWACK
THUNK
THUD
UNGH!

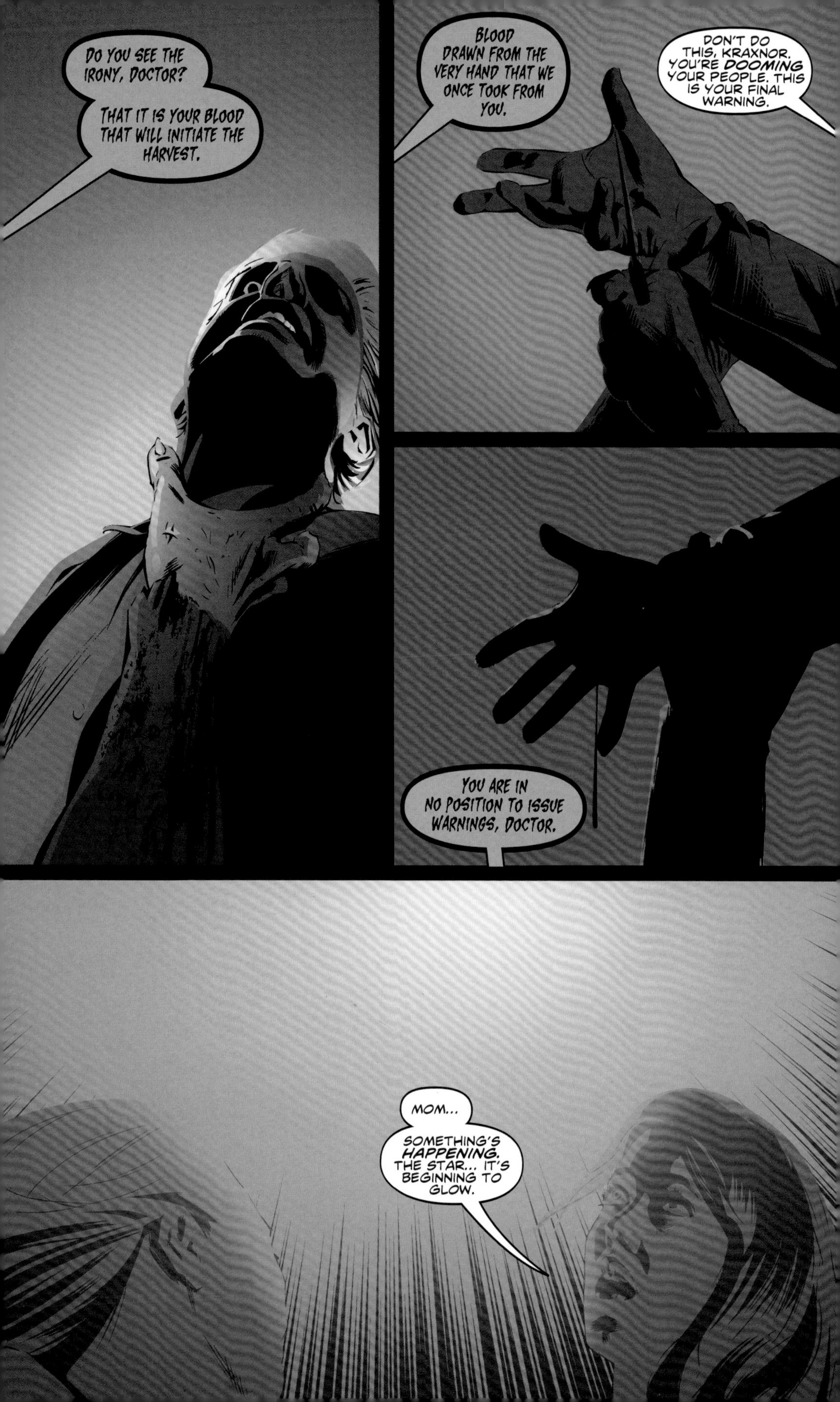
DO YOU SEE THE IRONY, DOCTOR?
THAT IT IS YOUR BLOOD THAT WILL INITIATE THE HARVEST.
BLOOD DRAWN FROM THE VERY HAND THAT WE ONCE TOOK FROM YOU.
DON'T DO THIS, KRAXNOR. YOU'RE DOOMING YOUR PEOPLE. THIS IS YOUR FINAL WARNING.
YOU ARE IN NO POSITION TO ISSUE WARNINGS, DOCTOR.
MOM...
SOMETHING'S HAPPENING. THE STAR... IT'S BEGINNING TO GLOW.

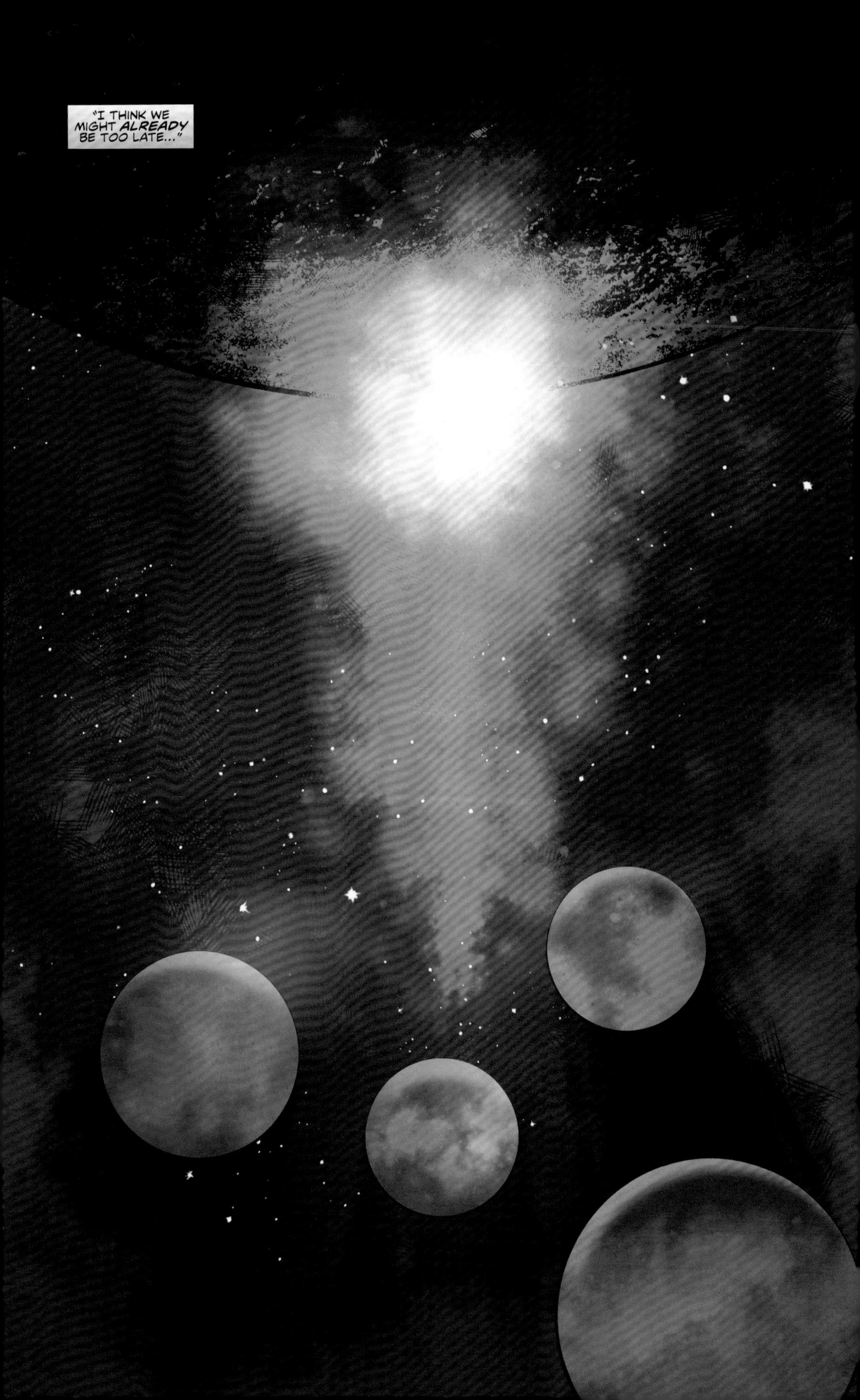
"I THINK WE MIGHT ALREADY BE TOO LATE..."

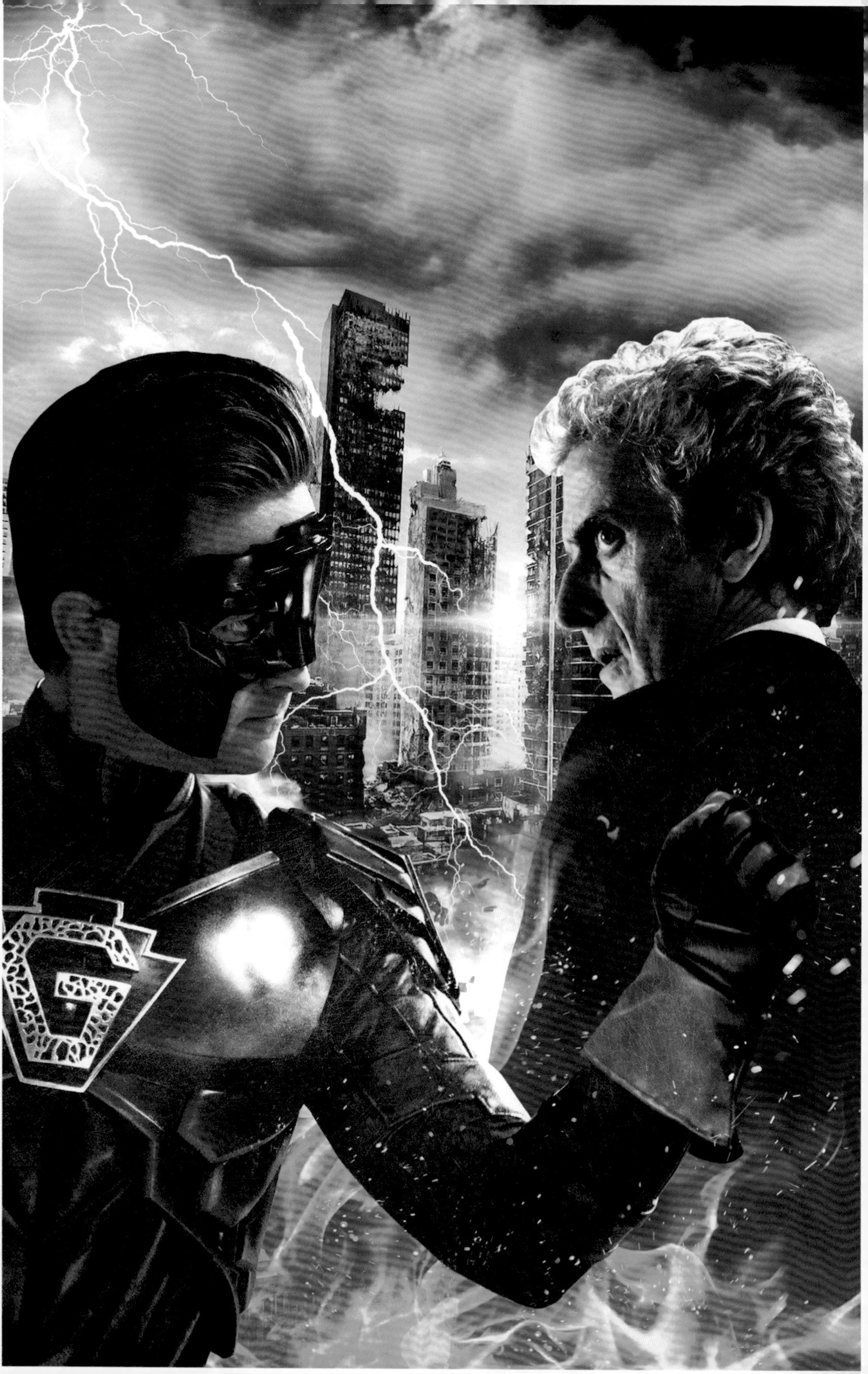

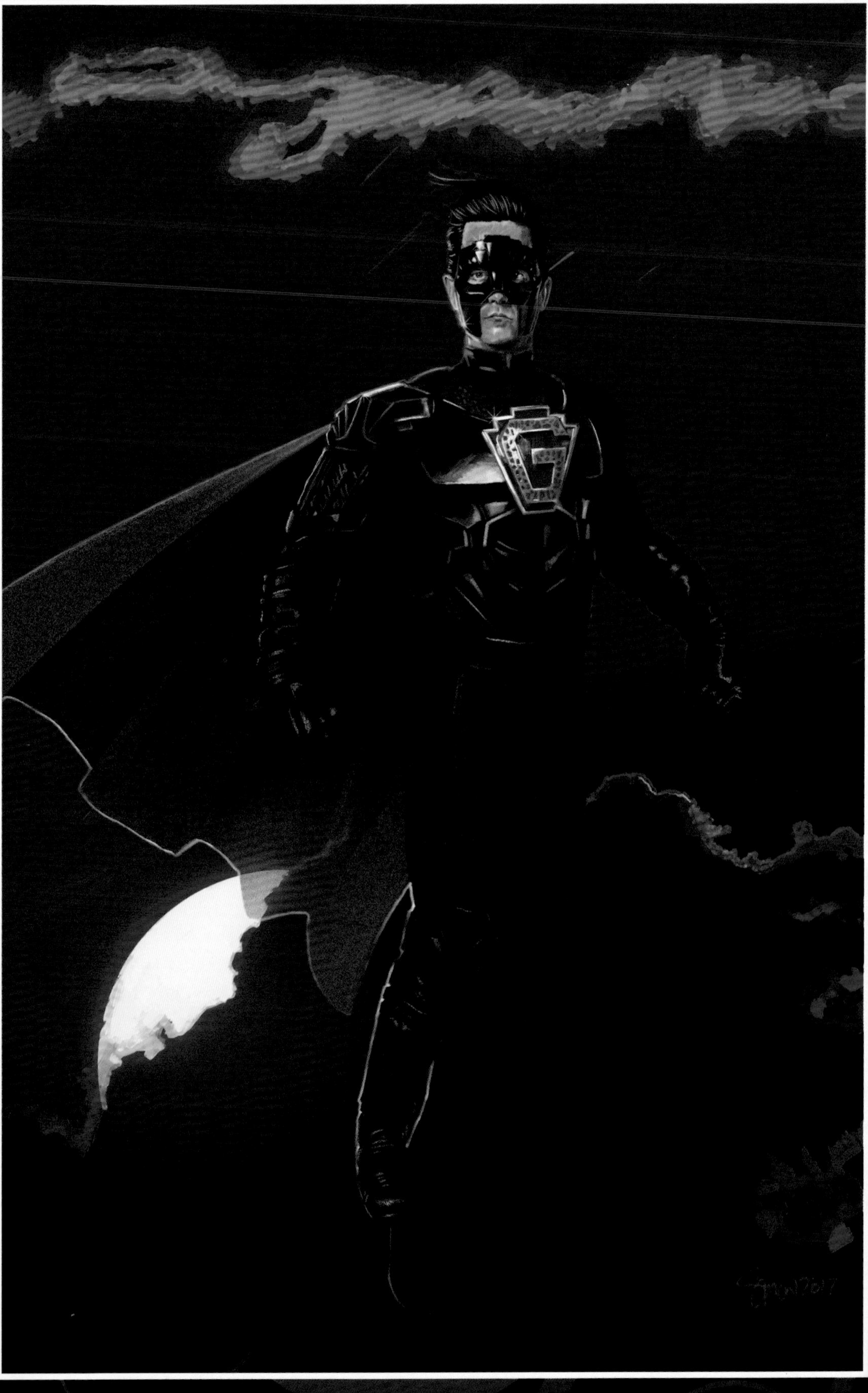

#4 Cover A: SIMON MYERS

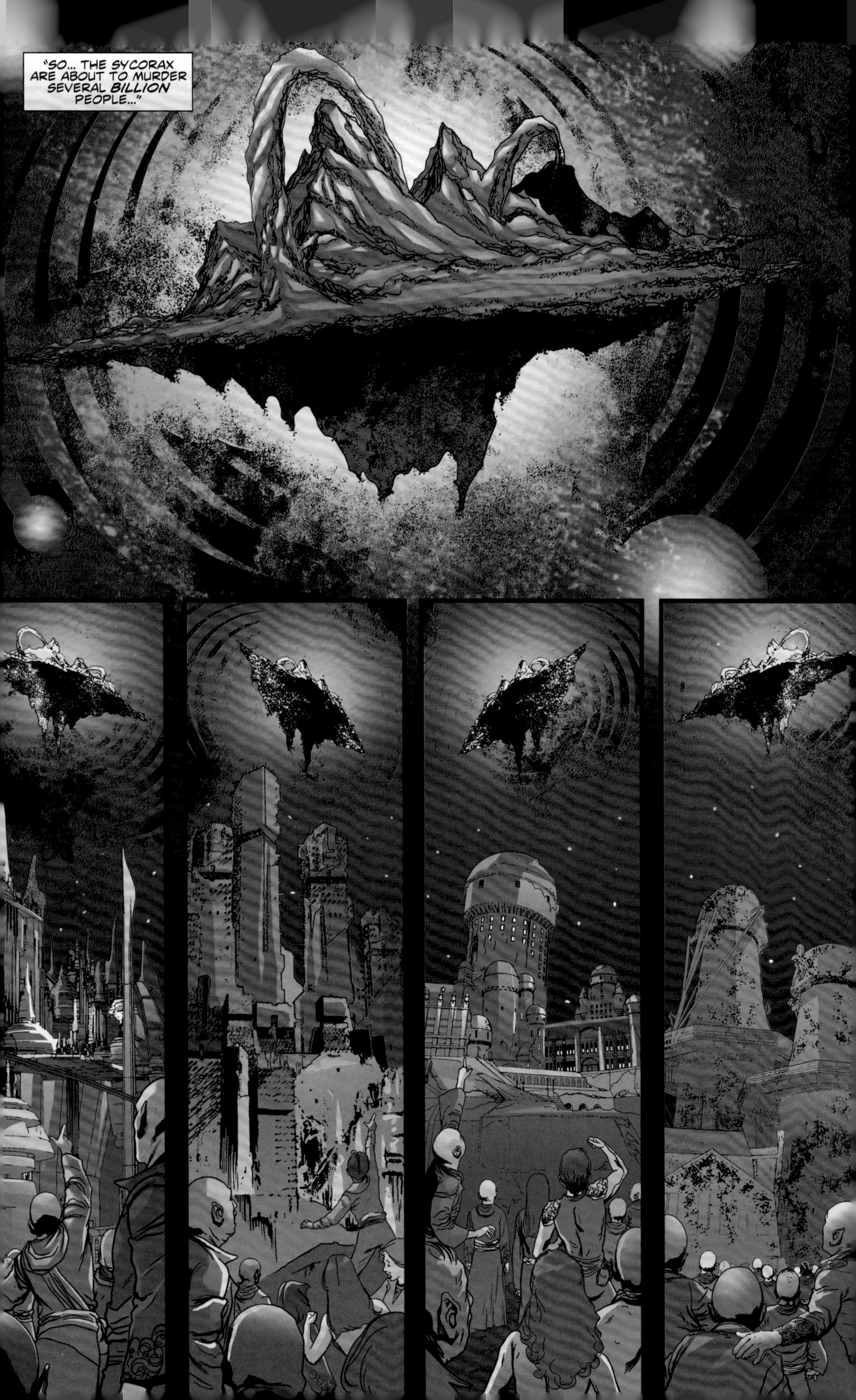
"SO... THE SYCORAX ARE ABOUT TO MURDER SEVERAL BILLION PEOPLE..."

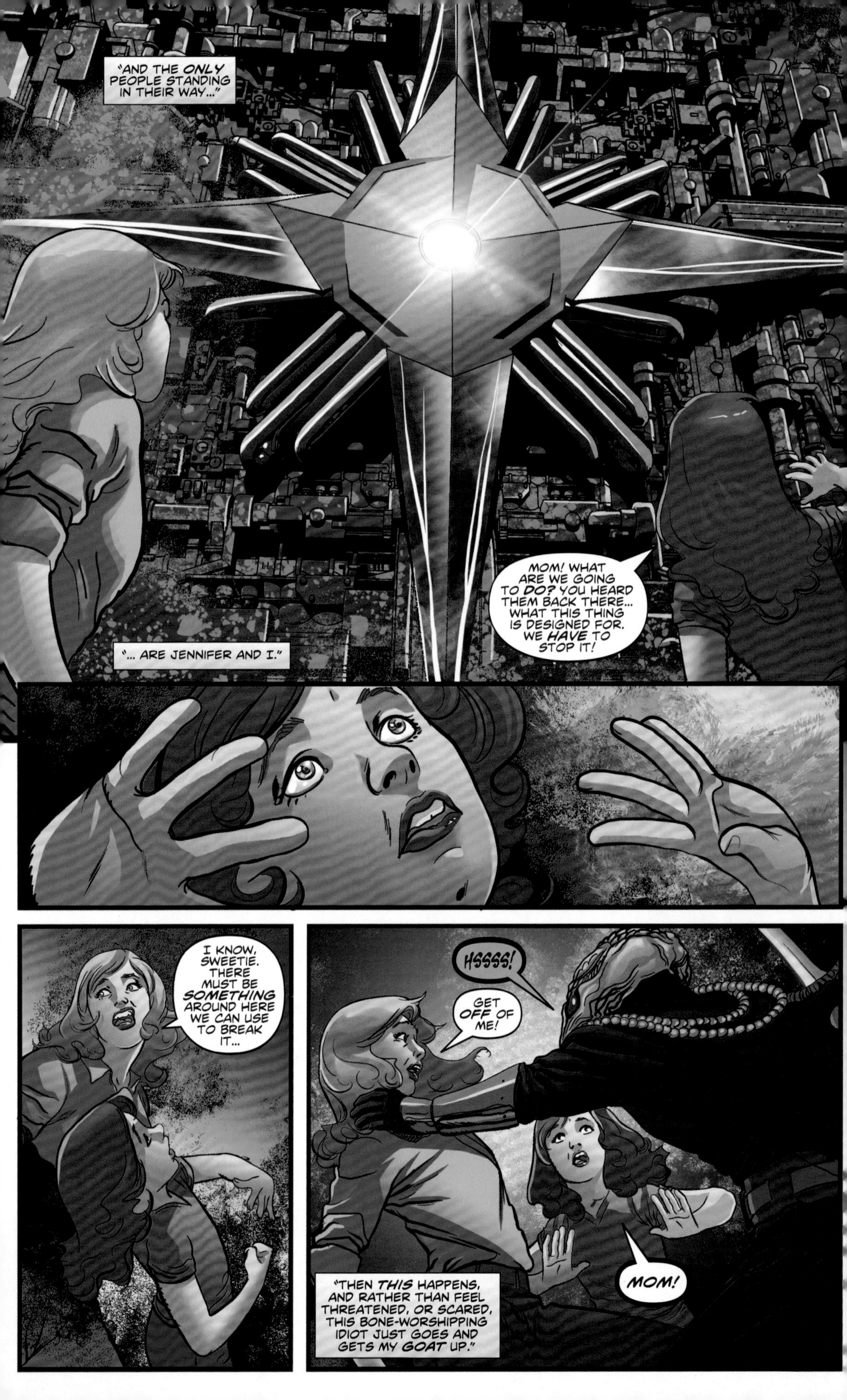

"AND THE ONLY PEOPLE STANDING IN THEIR WAY..."
"... ARE JENNIFER AND I."
MOM! WHAT ARE WE GOING TO DO? YOU HEARD THEM BACK THERE... WHAT THIS THING IS DESIGNED FOR. WE HAVE TO STOP IT!
I KNOW, SWEETIE. THERE MUST BE SOMETHING AROUND HERE WE CAN USE TO BREAK IT...
HSSSS!
GET OFF OF ME!
MOM!
"THEN THIS HAPPENS, AND RATHER THAN FEEL THREATENED, OR SCARED, THIS BONE-WORSHIPPING IDIOT JUST GOES AND GETS MY GOAT UP."

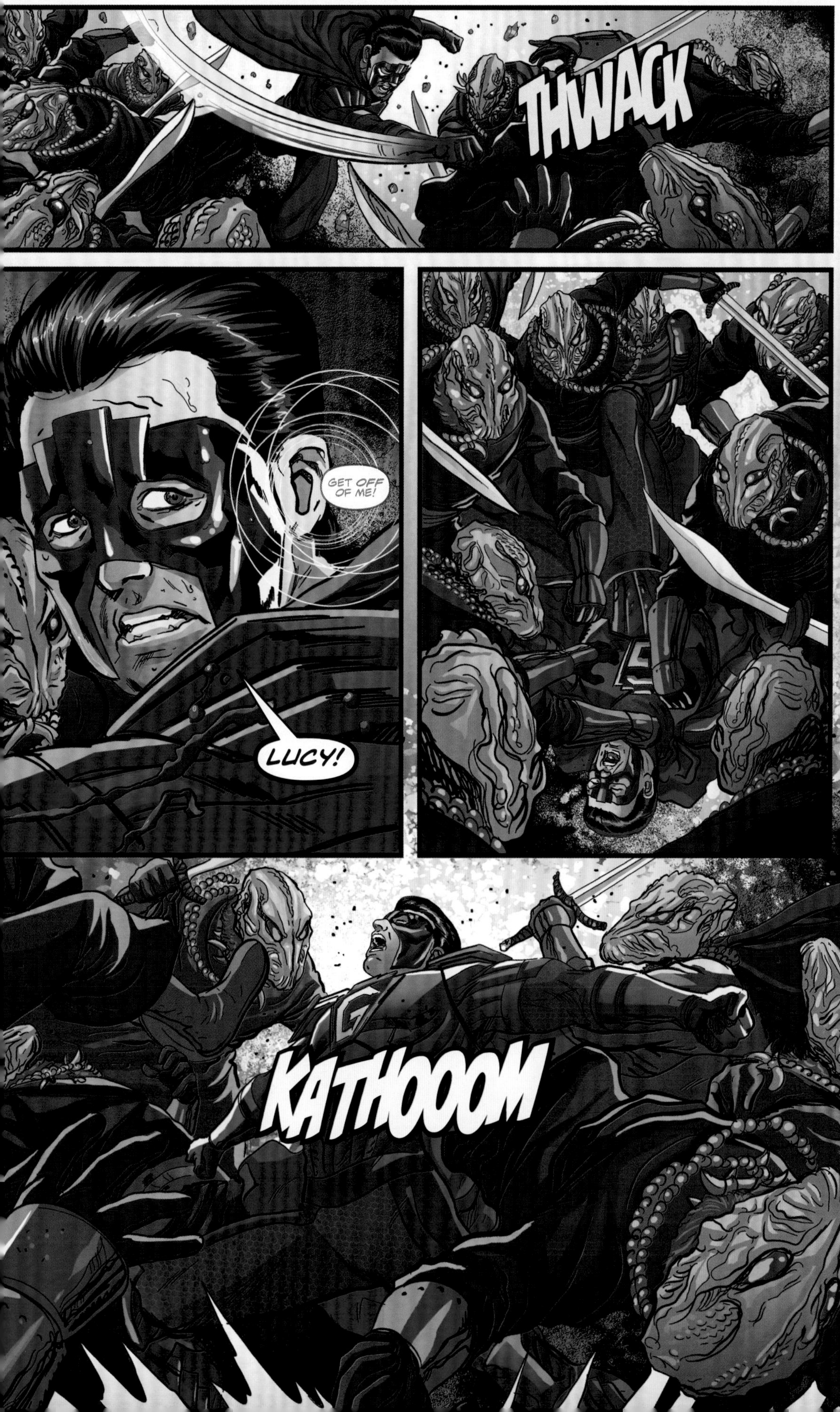
THWACK
GET OFF OF ME!
LUCY!
KATHOOOM

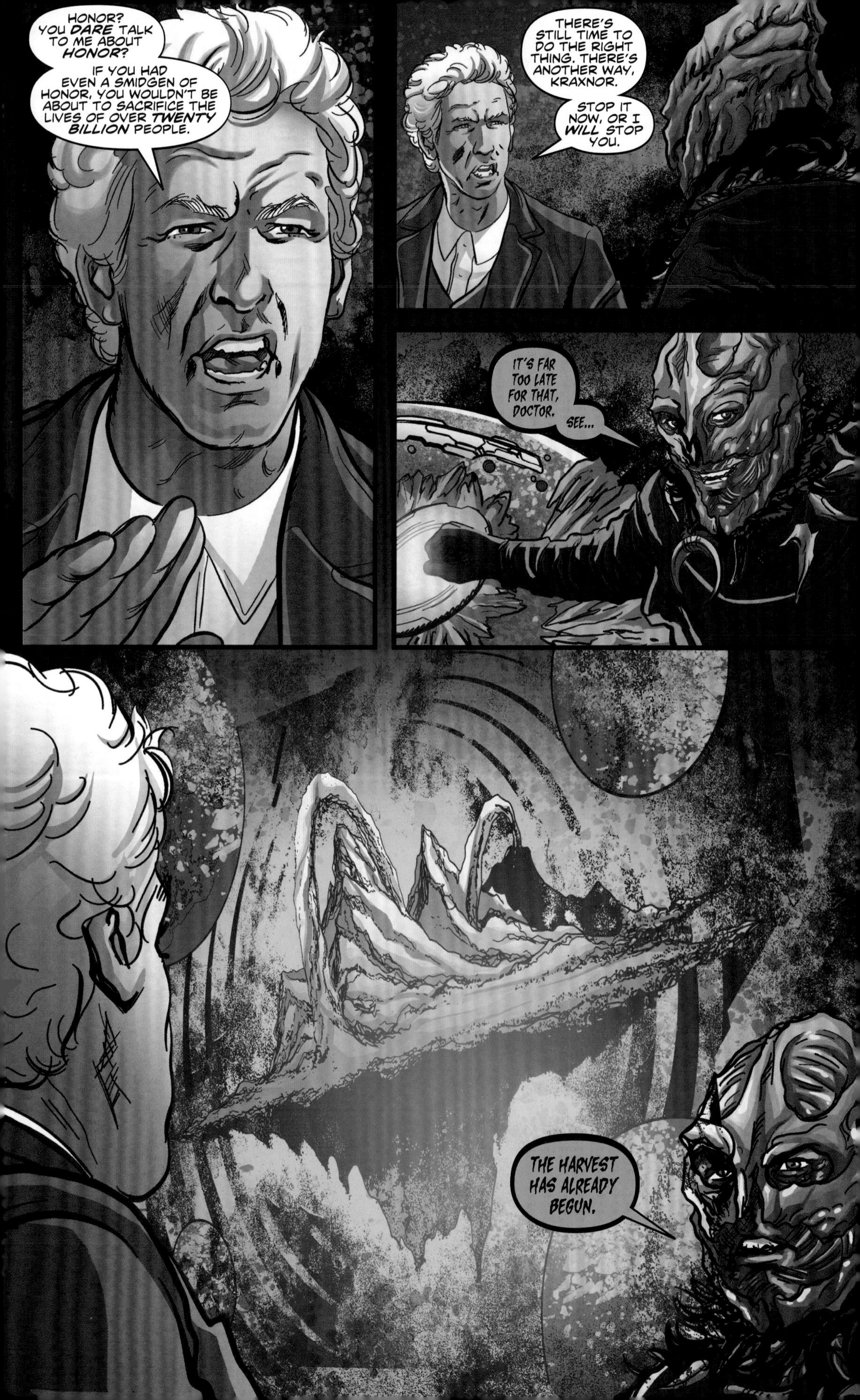
HONOR? YOU DARE TALK TO ME ABOUT HONOR?
IF YOU HAD EVEN A SMIDGEN OF HONOR, YOU WOULDN'T BE ABOUT TO SACRIFICE THE LIVES OF OVER TWENTY BILLION PEOPLE.
THERE'S STILL TIME TO DO THE RIGHT THING. THERE'S ANOTHER WAY, KRAXNOR.
STOP IT NOW, OR I WILL STOP YOU.
IT'S FAR TOO LATE FOR THAT, DOCTOR.
SEE...
THE HARVEST HAS ALREADY BEGUN.

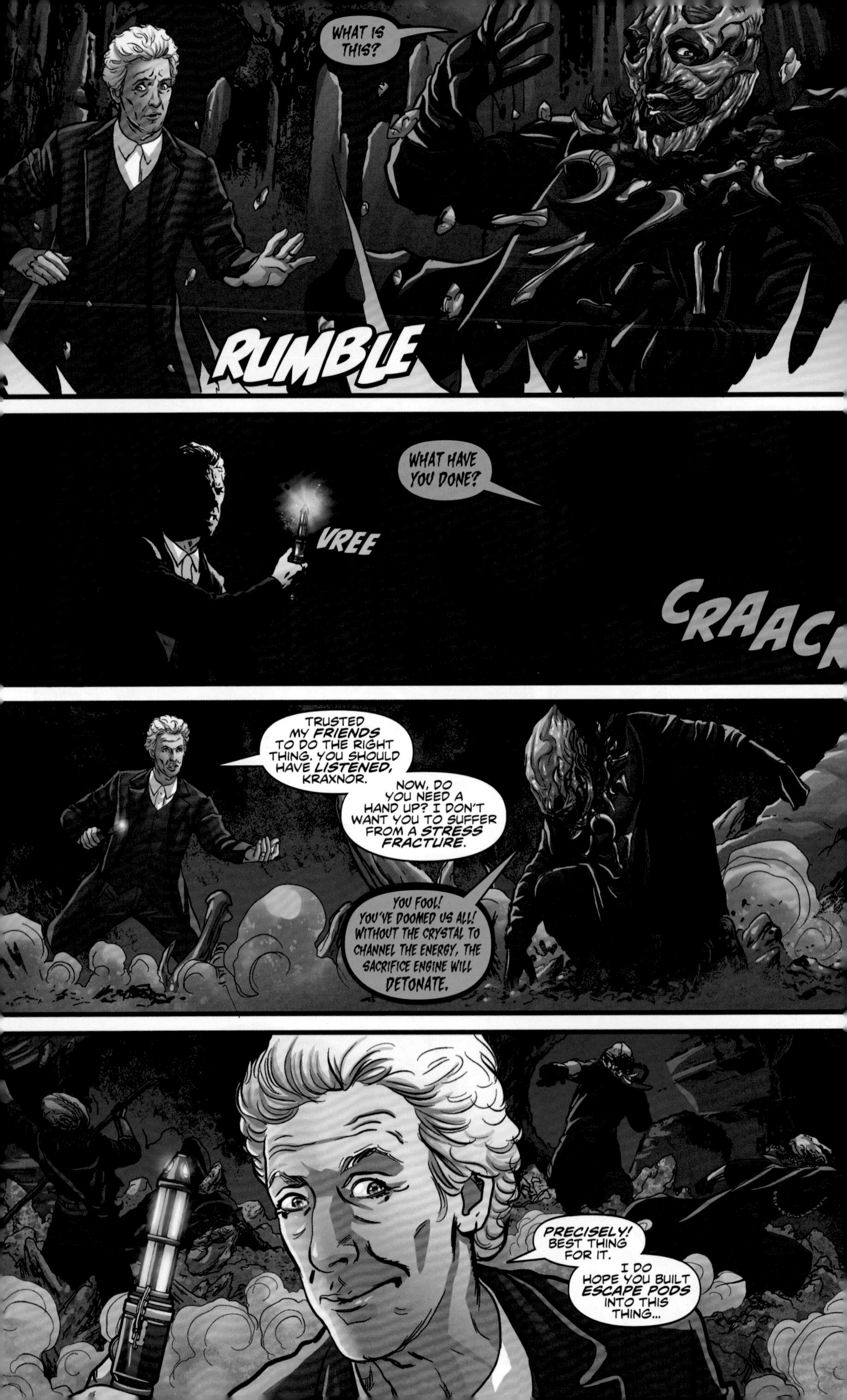
WHAT IS THIS?
RUMBLE
WHAT HAVE YOU DONE?
VREE
CRAACK
TRUSTED MY FRIENDS TO DO THE RIGHT THING. YOU SHOULD HAVE LISTENED, KRAXNOR.
NOW, DO YOU NEED A HAND UP? I DON'T WANT YOU TO SUFFER FROM A STRESS FRACTURE.
YOU FOOL! YOU'VE DOOMED US ALL! WITHOUT THE CRYSTAL TO CHANNEL THE ENERGY, THE SACRIFICE ENGINE WILL DETONATE.
PRECISELY! BEST THING FOR IT.
I DO HOPE YOU BUILT ESCAPE PODS INTO THIS THING...

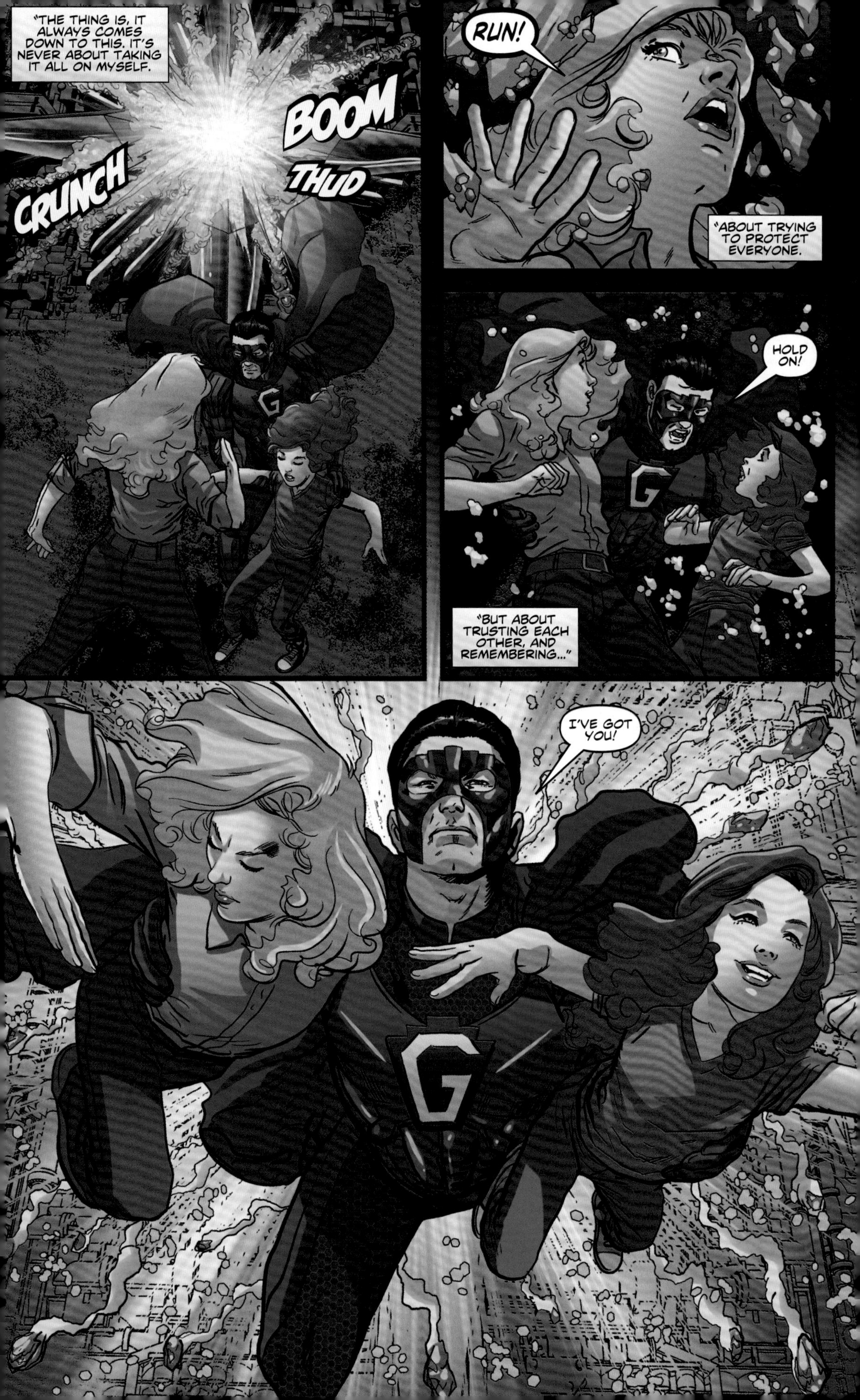
"THE THING IS, IT ALWAYS COMES DOWN TO THIS. IT'S NEVER ABOUT TAKING IT ALL ON MYSELF.
BOOM
CRUNCH
THUD
RUN!
"ABOUT TRYING TO PROTECT EVERYONE.
HOLD ON!
"BUT ABOUT TRUSTING EACH OTHER, AND REMEMBERING..."
I'VE GOT YOU!

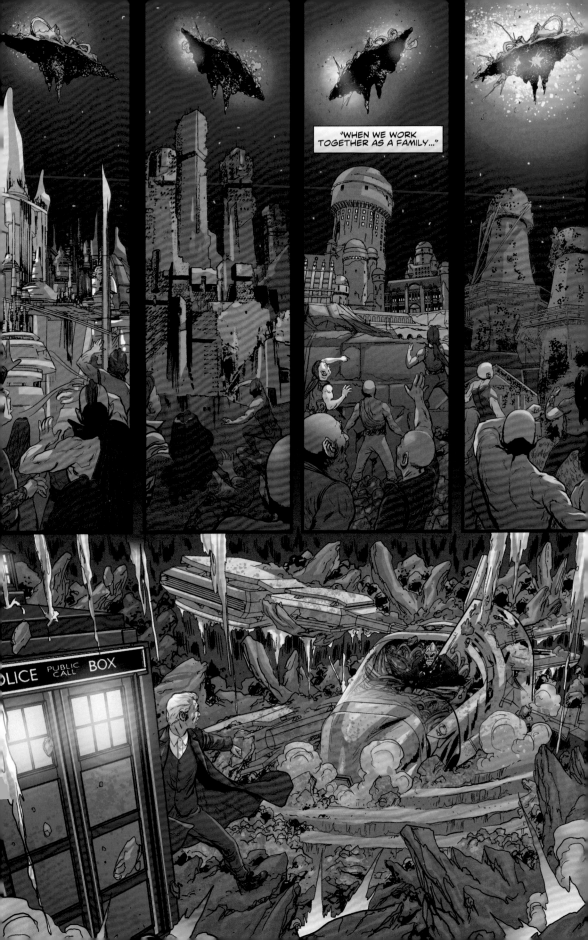

"WHEN WE WORK TOGETHER AS A FAMILY..."

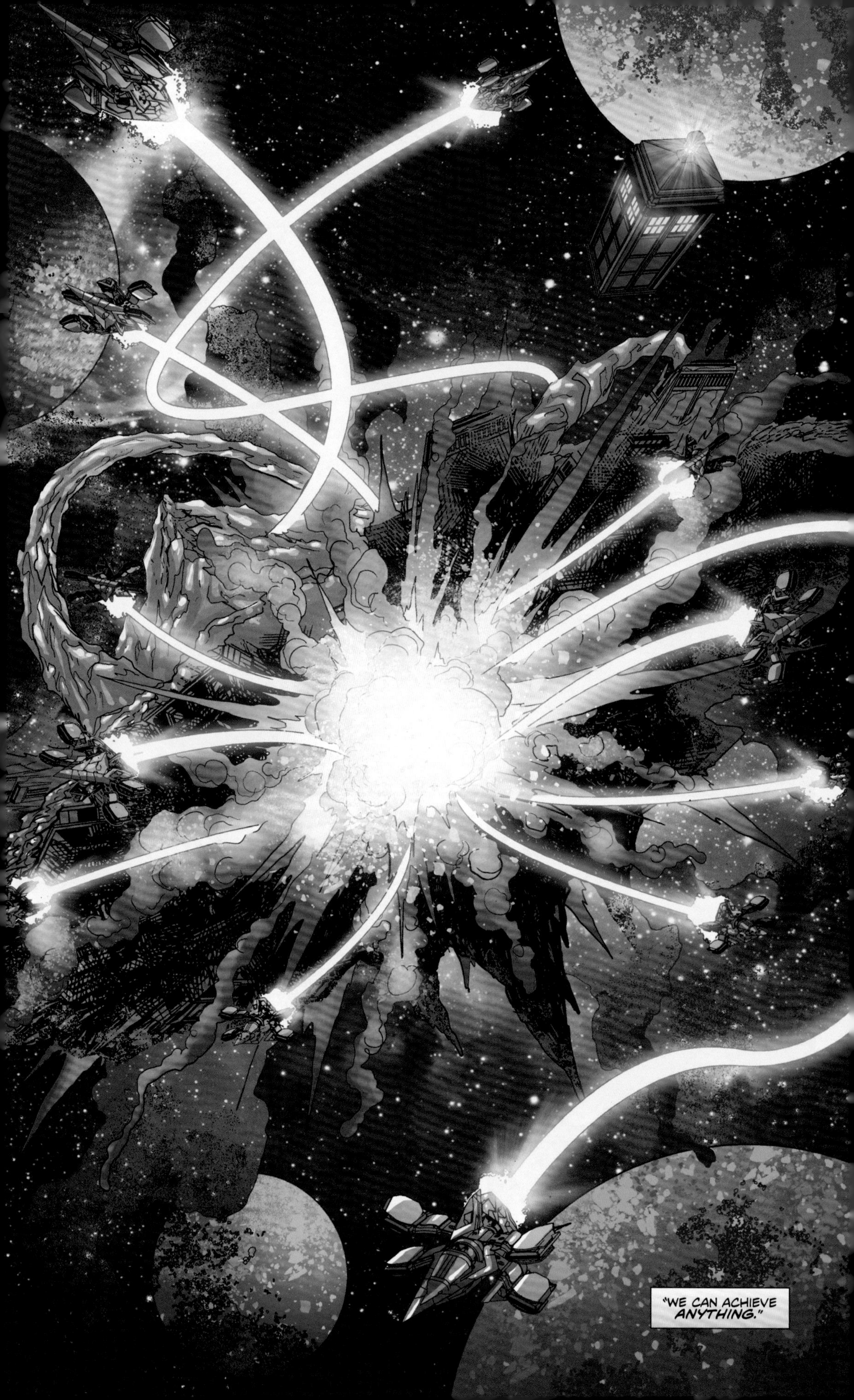
"WE CAN ACHIEVE
ANYTHING."

WELL, I CAN'T SAY I'M SORRY THAT'S OVER.

YOU'VE GOT ALL THE MISSING CRYSTALS NOW, DOCTOR.

WHAT NOW? YOU STILL HAVEN'T TOLD US WHAT YOU'RE GOING TO DO WITH THEM.

APART FROM SAVE THE UNIVERSE, YOU MEAN?

DOCTOR...

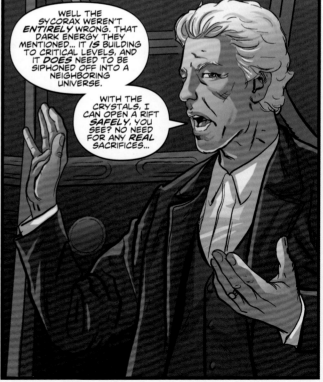

WELL THE SYCORAX WEREN'T ENTIRELY WRONG. THAT DARK ENERGY THEY MENTIONED... IT IS BUILDING TO CRITICAL LEVELS, AND IT DOES NEED TO BE SIPHONED OFF INTO A NEIGHBORING UNIVERSE.

WITH THE CRYSTALS, I CAN OPEN A RIFT SAFELY, YOU SEE? NO NEED FOR ANY REAL SACRIFICES...

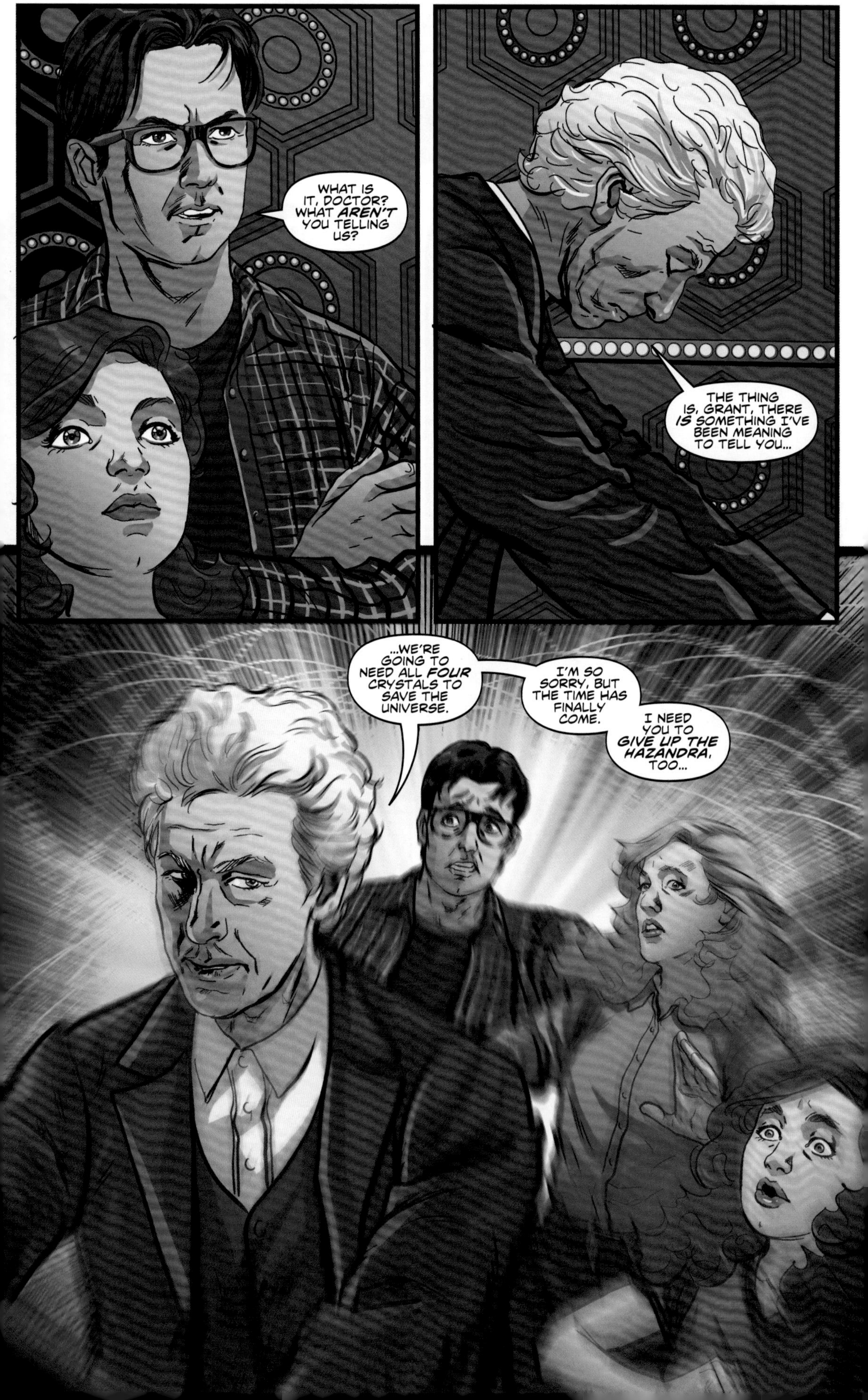
WHAT IS IT, DOCTOR? WHAT *AREN'T* YOU TELLING US?
THE THING IS, GRANT, THERE *IS* SOMETHING I'VE BEEN MEANING TO TELL YOU...
...WE'RE GOING TO NEED ALL *FOUR* CRYSTALS TO SAVE THE UNIVERSE.
I'M SO SORRY, BUT THE TIME HAS FINALLY COME.
I NEED YOU TO *GIVE UP THE HAZANDRA*, TOO...

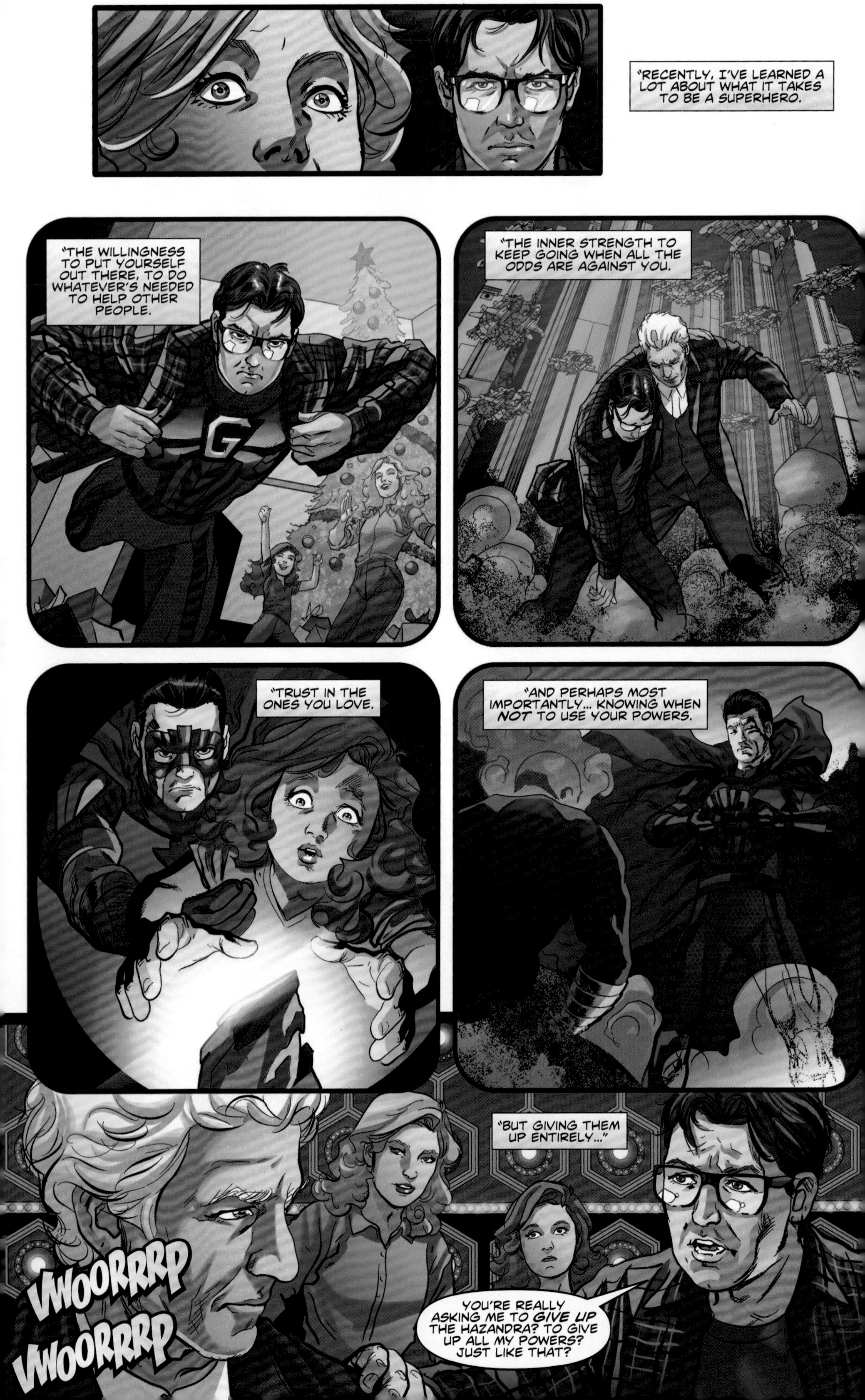
"RECENTLY, I'VE LEARNED A LOT ABOUT WHAT IT TAKES TO BE A SUPERHERO.
"THE WILLINGNESS TO PUT YOURSELF OUT THERE, TO DO WHATEVER'S NEEDED TO HELP OTHER PEOPLE.
"THE INNER STRENGTH TO KEEP GOING WHEN ALL THE ODDS ARE AGAINST YOU.
"TRUST IN THE ONES YOU LOVE.
"AND PERHAPS MOST IMPORTANTLY... KNOWING WHEN NOT TO USE YOUR POWERS.
"BUT GIVING THEM UP ENTIRELY..."
VWOORRRP
VWOORRRP
YOU'RE REALLY ASKING ME TO GIVE UP THE HAZANDRA? TO GIVE UP ALL MY POWERS? JUST LIKE THAT?

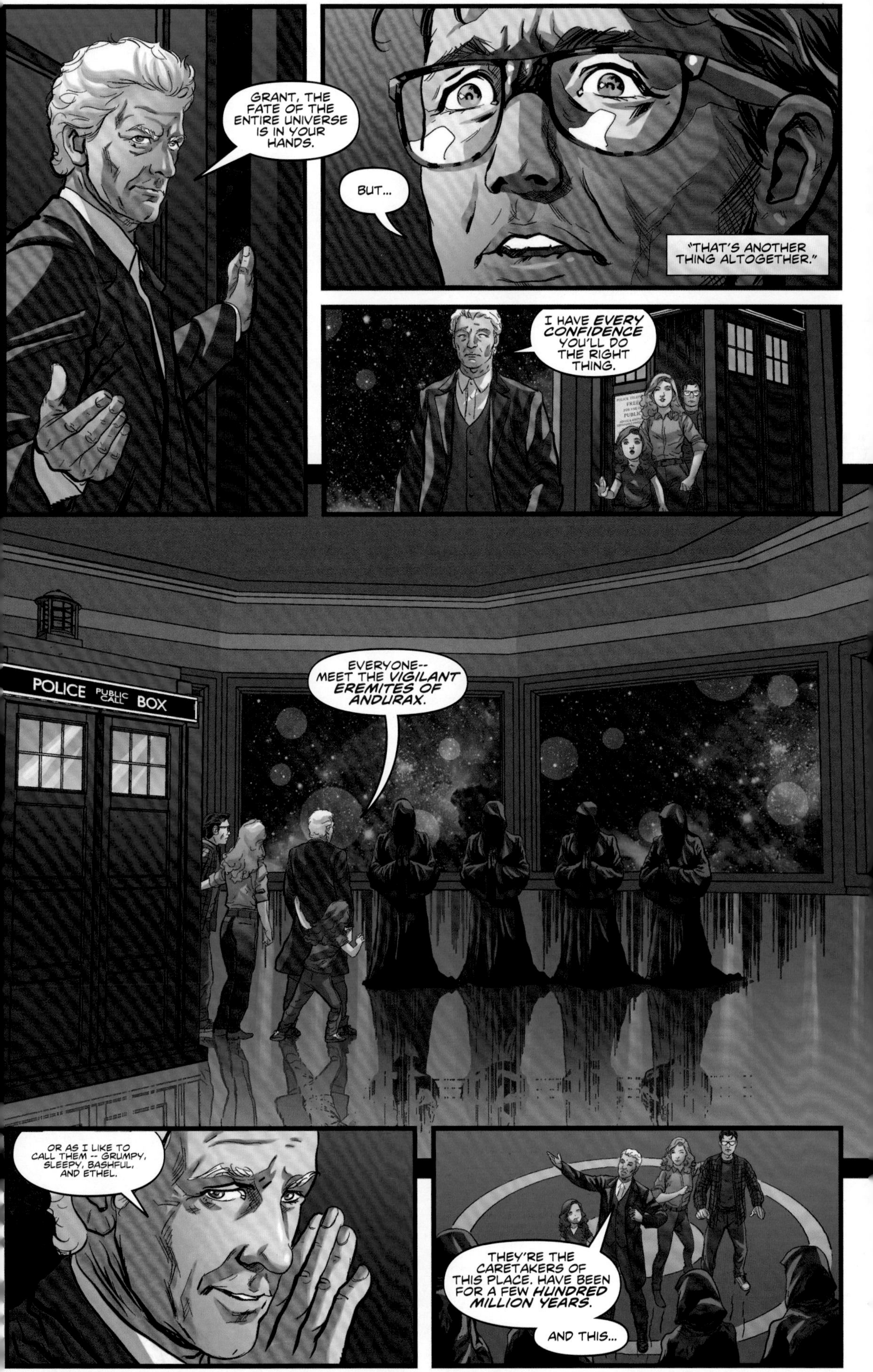
GRANT, THE FATE OF THE ENTIRE UNIVERSE IS IN YOUR HANDS.
BUT...
"THAT'S ANOTHER THING ALTOGETHER."
I HAVE EVERY CONFIDENCE YOU'LL DO THE RIGHT THING.
POLICE PUBLIC CALL BOX
EVERYONE-- MEET THE VIGILANT EREMITES OF ANDURAX.
OR AS I LIKE TO CALL THEM -- GRUMPY, SLEEPY, BASHFUL, AND ETHEL.
THEY'RE THE CARETAKERS OF THIS PLACE. HAVE BEEN FOR A FEW HUNDRED MILLION YEARS.
AND THIS...

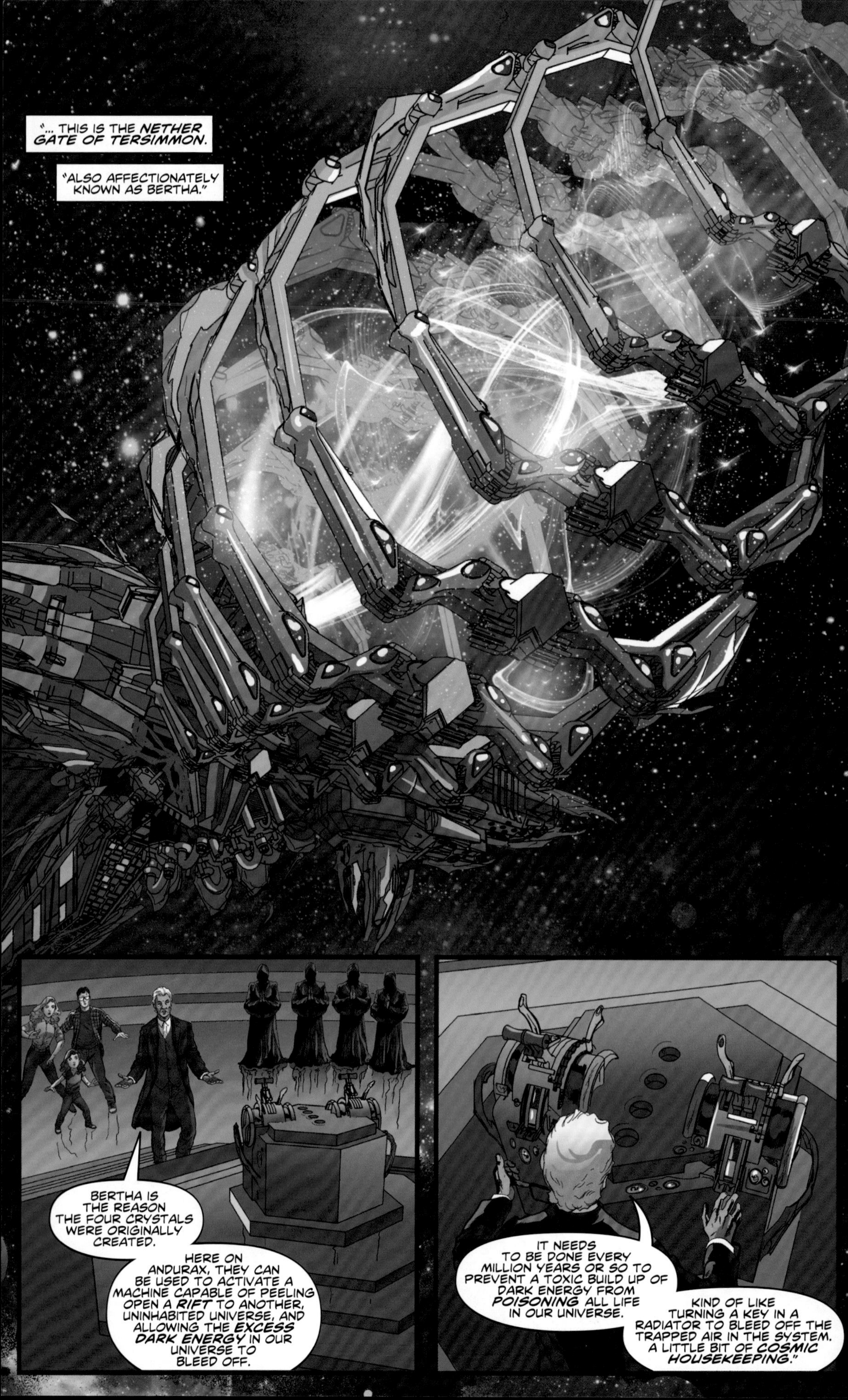
"... THIS IS THE NETHER GATE OF TERSIMMON.
"ALSO AFFECTIONATELY KNOWN AS BERTHA."
BERTHA IS THE REASON THE FOUR CRYSTALS WERE ORIGINALLY CREATED.
HERE ON ANDURAX, THEY CAN BE USED TO ACTIVATE A MACHINE CAPABLE OF PEELING OPEN A RIFT TO ANOTHER, UNINHABITED UNIVERSE, AND ALLOWING THE EXCESS DARK ENERGY IN OUR UNIVERSE TO BLEED OFF.
IT NEEDS TO BE DONE EVERY MILLION YEARS OR SO TO PREVENT A TOXIC BUILD UP OF DARK ENERGY FROM POISONING ALL LIFE IN OUR UNIVERSE.
KIND OF LIKE TURNING A KEY IN A RADIATOR TO BLEED OFF THE TRAPPED AIR IN THE SYSTEM. A LITTLE BIT OF COSMIC HOUSEKEEPING."

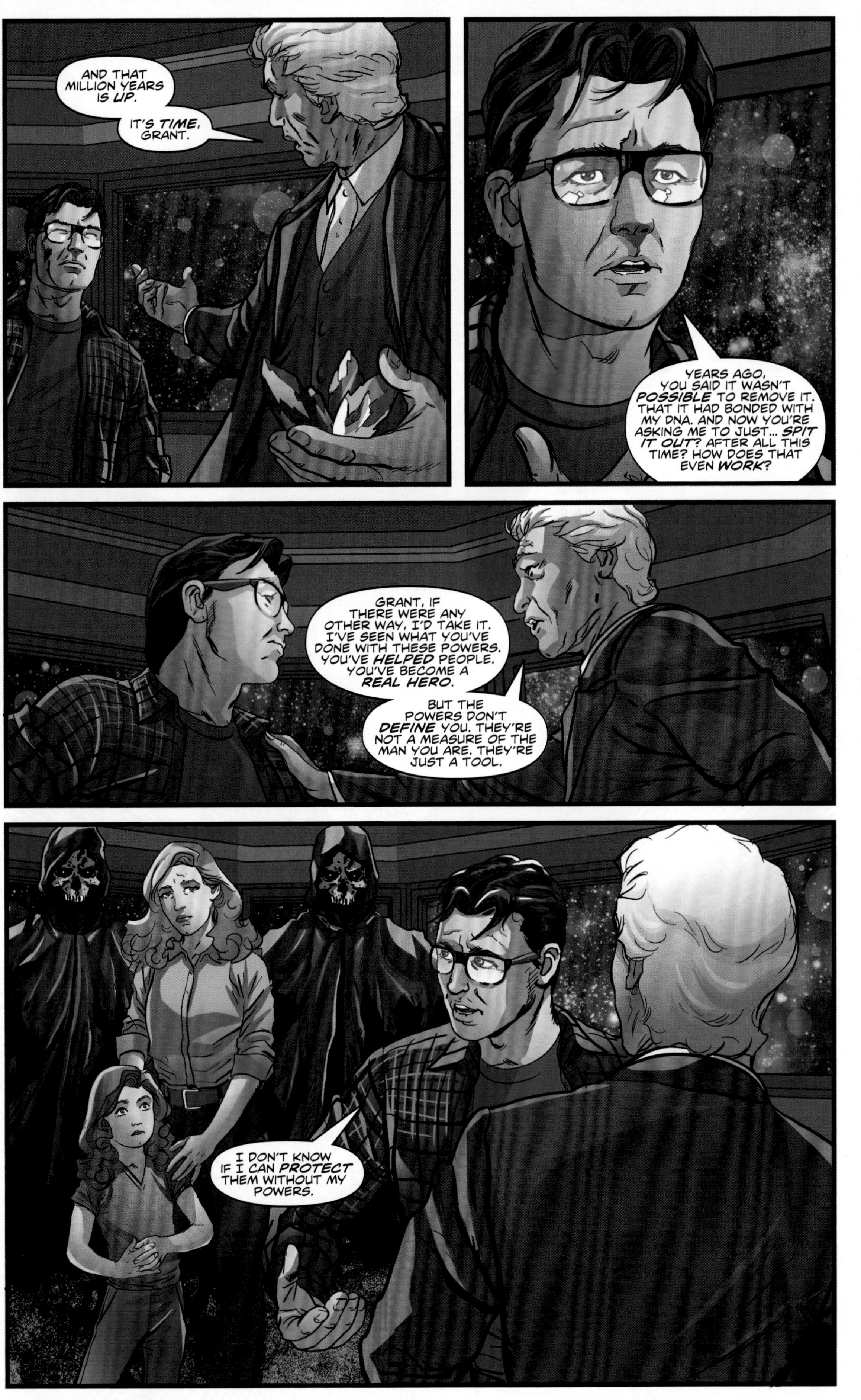

AND THAT MILLION YEARS IS UP.
IT'S TIME, GRANT.
YEARS AGO, YOU SAID IT WASN'T POSSIBLE TO REMOVE IT. THAT IT HAD BONDED WITH MY DNA. AND NOW YOU'RE ASKING ME TO JUST... SPIT IT OUT? AFTER ALL THIS TIME? HOW DOES THAT EVEN WORK?
GRANT, IF THERE WERE ANY OTHER WAY, I'D TAKE IT. I'VE SEEN WHAT YOU'VE DONE WITH THESE POWERS. YOU'VE HELPED PEOPLE. YOU'VE BECOME A REAL HERO.
BUT THE POWERS DON'T DEFINE YOU. THEY'RE NOT A MEASURE OF THE MAN YOU ARE. THEY'RE JUST A TOOL.
I DON'T KNOW IF I CAN PROTECT THEM WITHOUT MY POWERS.

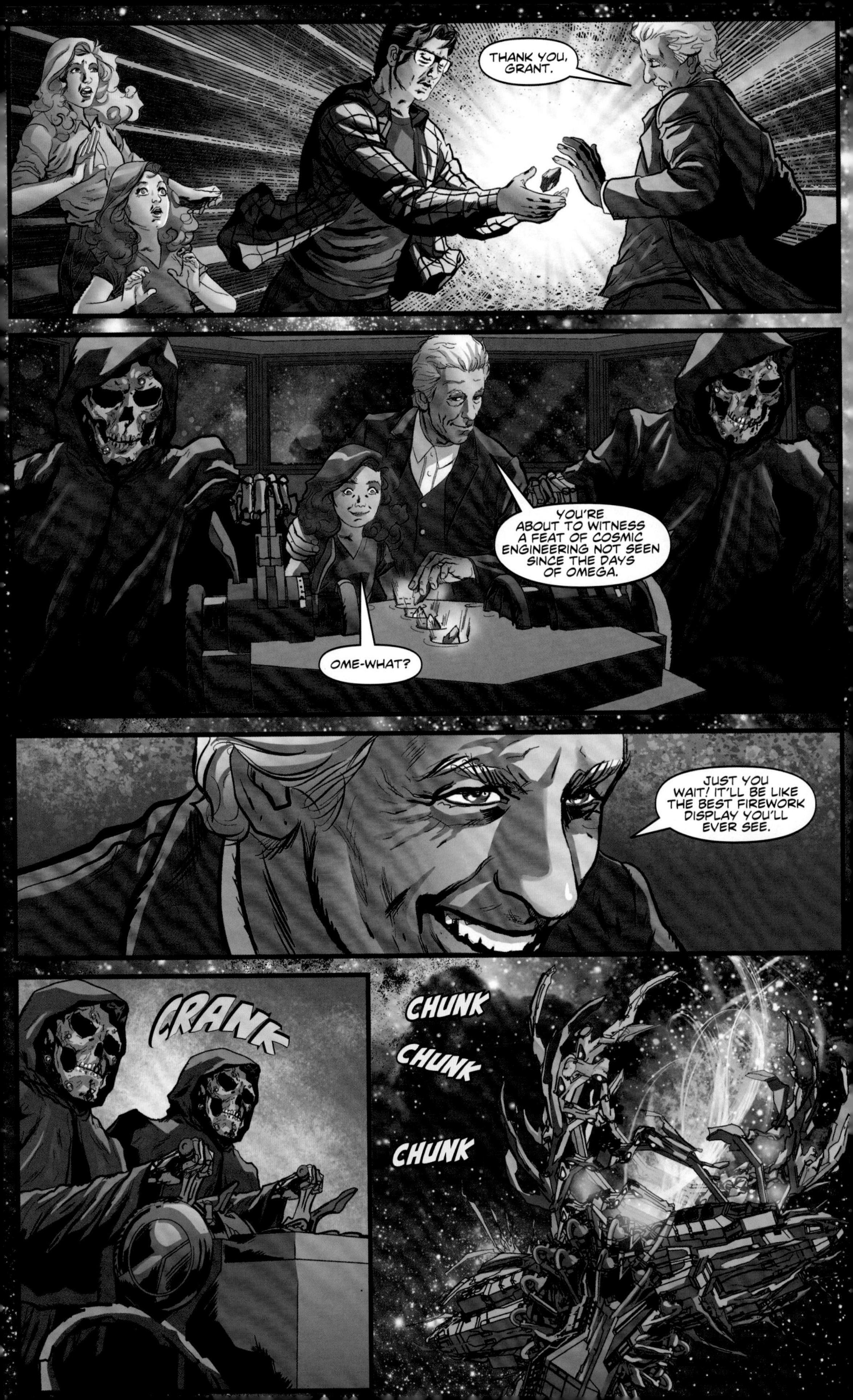
THANK YOU, GRANT.
YOU'RE ABOUT TO WITNESS A FEAT OF COSMIC ENGINEERING NOT SEEN SINCE THE DAYS OF OMEGA.
OME-WHAT?
JUST YOU WAIT! IT'LL BE LIKE THE BEST FIREWORK DISPLAY YOU'LL EVER SEE.
CRANK
CHUNK
CHUNK
CHUNK

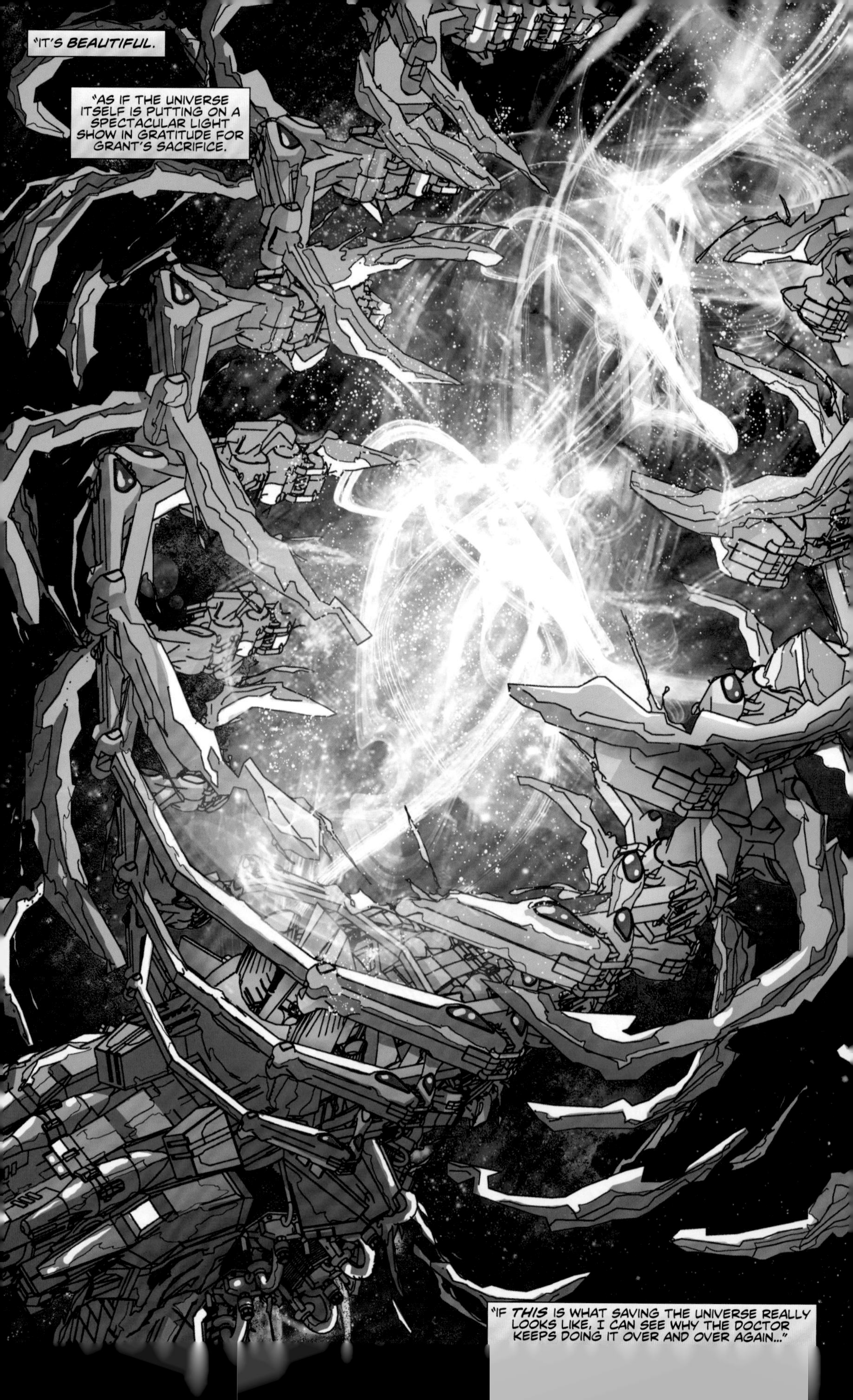
"IT'S *BEAUTIFUL*.
"AS IF THE UNIVERSE ITSELF IS PUTTING ON A SPECTACULAR LIGHT SHOW IN GRATITUDE FOR GRANT'S SACRIFICE.
"IF *THIS* IS WHAT SAVING THE UNIVERSE REALLY LOOKS LIKE, I CAN SEE WHY THE DOCTOR KEEPS DOING IT OVER AND OVER AGAIN..."

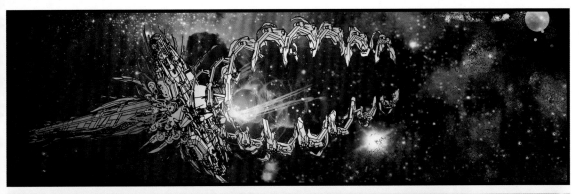

CHUNK
CHUNK
CHUNK

IT'S DONE.

JUST LIKE THAT?

JUST LIKE THAT. FOR ANOTHER MILLION YEARS, AT LEAST.

SEE YOU NEXT TIME, ETHEL.

VWOORRRP

VWOORRRP

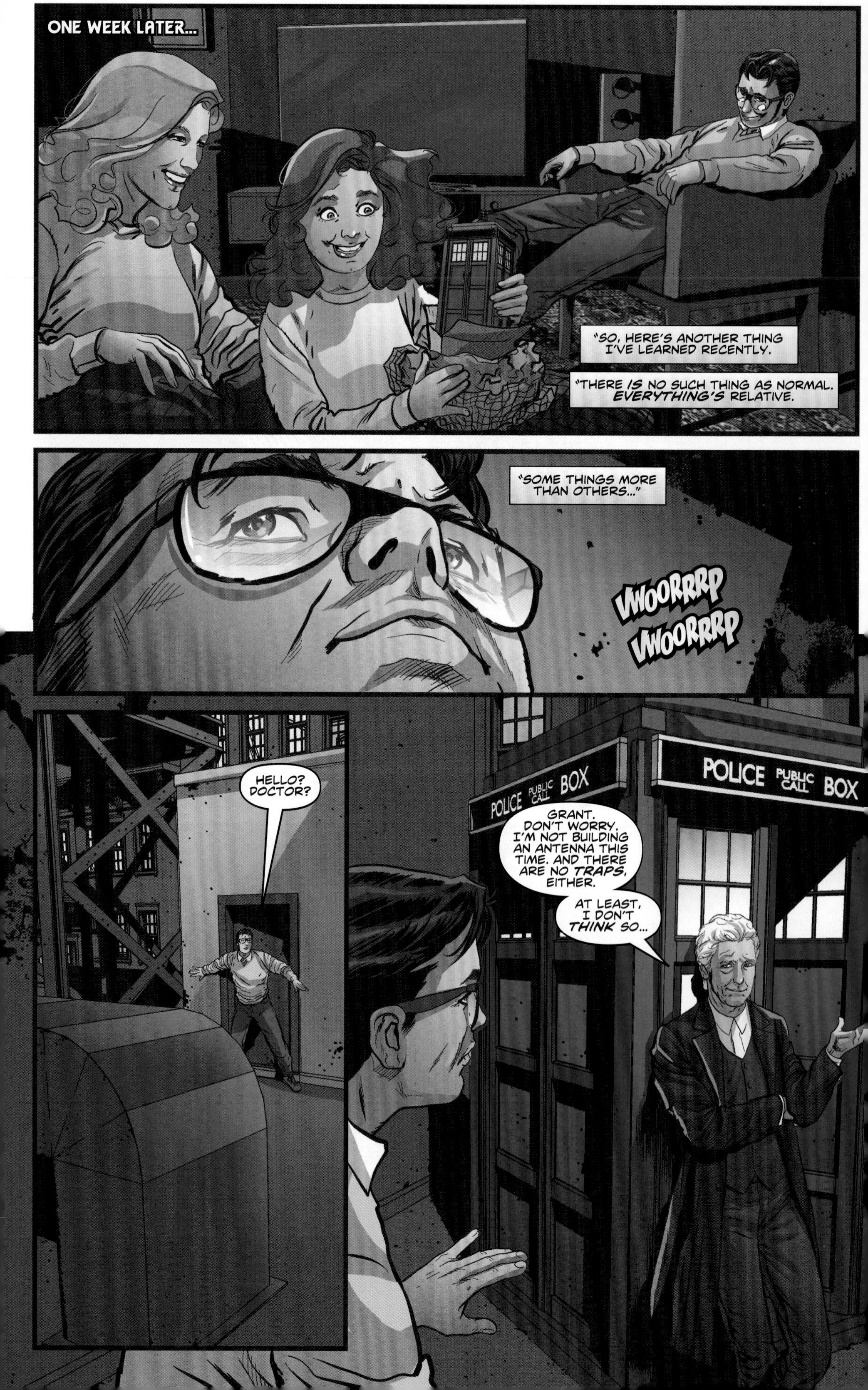
ONE WEEK LATER...
"SO, HERE'S ANOTHER THING I'VE LEARNED RECENTLY.
"THERE IS NO SUCH THING AS NORMAL. EVERYTHING'S RELATIVE.
"SOME THINGS MORE THAN OTHERS..."
VWOORRRP VWOORRRP
HELLO? DOCTOR?
POLICE PUBLIC CALL BOX
POLICE PUBLIC CALL BOX
GRANT. DON'T WORRY. I'M NOT BUILDING AN ANTENNA THIS TIME. AND THERE ARE NO TRAPS, EITHER.
AT LEAST, I DON'T THINK SO...

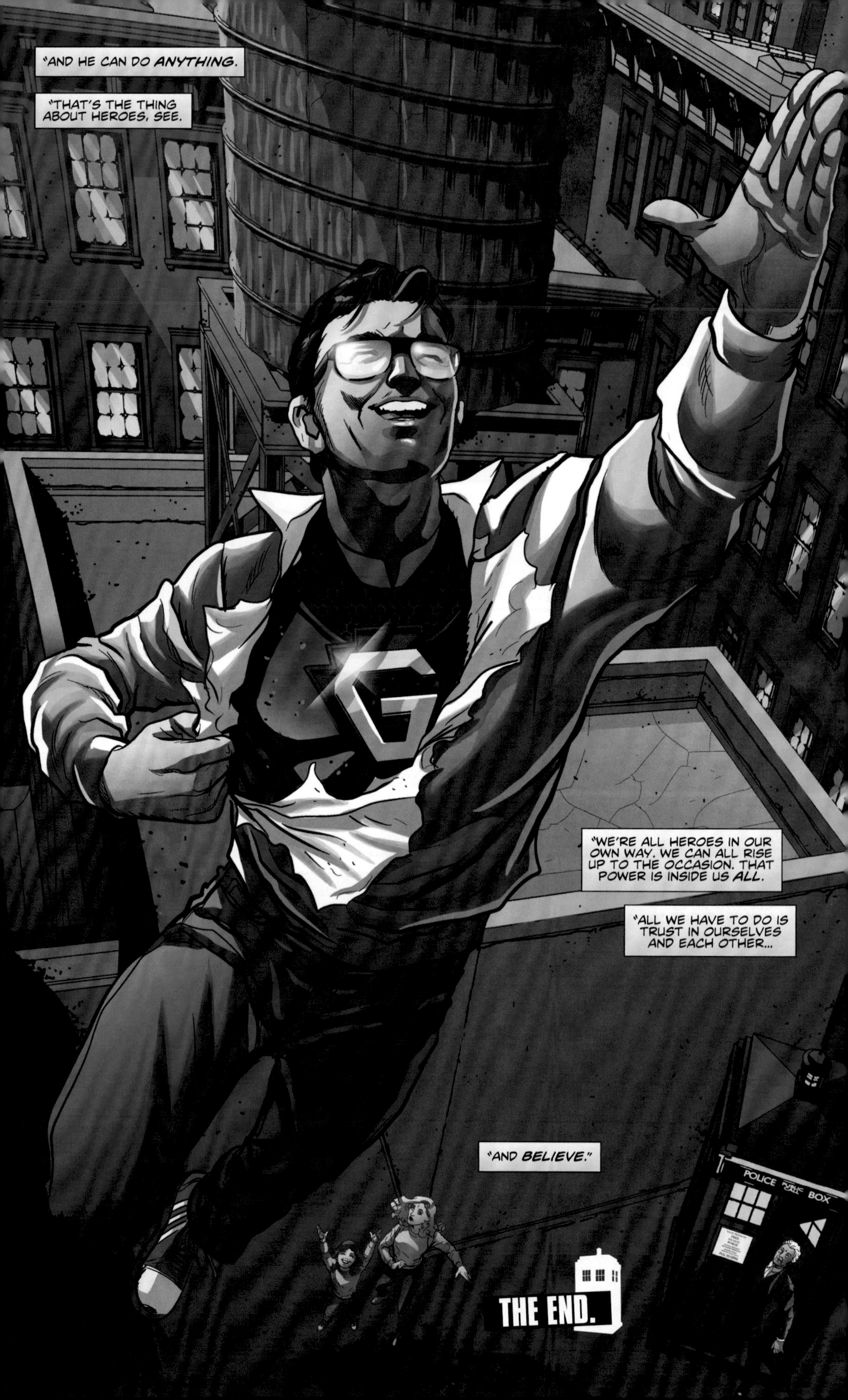
"AND HE CAN DO *ANYTHING*.
"THAT'S THE THING ABOUT HEROES, SEE.
"WE'RE ALL HEROES IN OUR OWN WAY. WE CAN ALL RISE UP TO THE OCCASION. THAT POWER IS INSIDE US *ALL*.
"ALL WE HAVE TO DO IS TRUST IN OURSELVES AND EACH OTHER...
"AND *BELIEVE*."
POLICE PUBLIC CALL BOX
THE END.

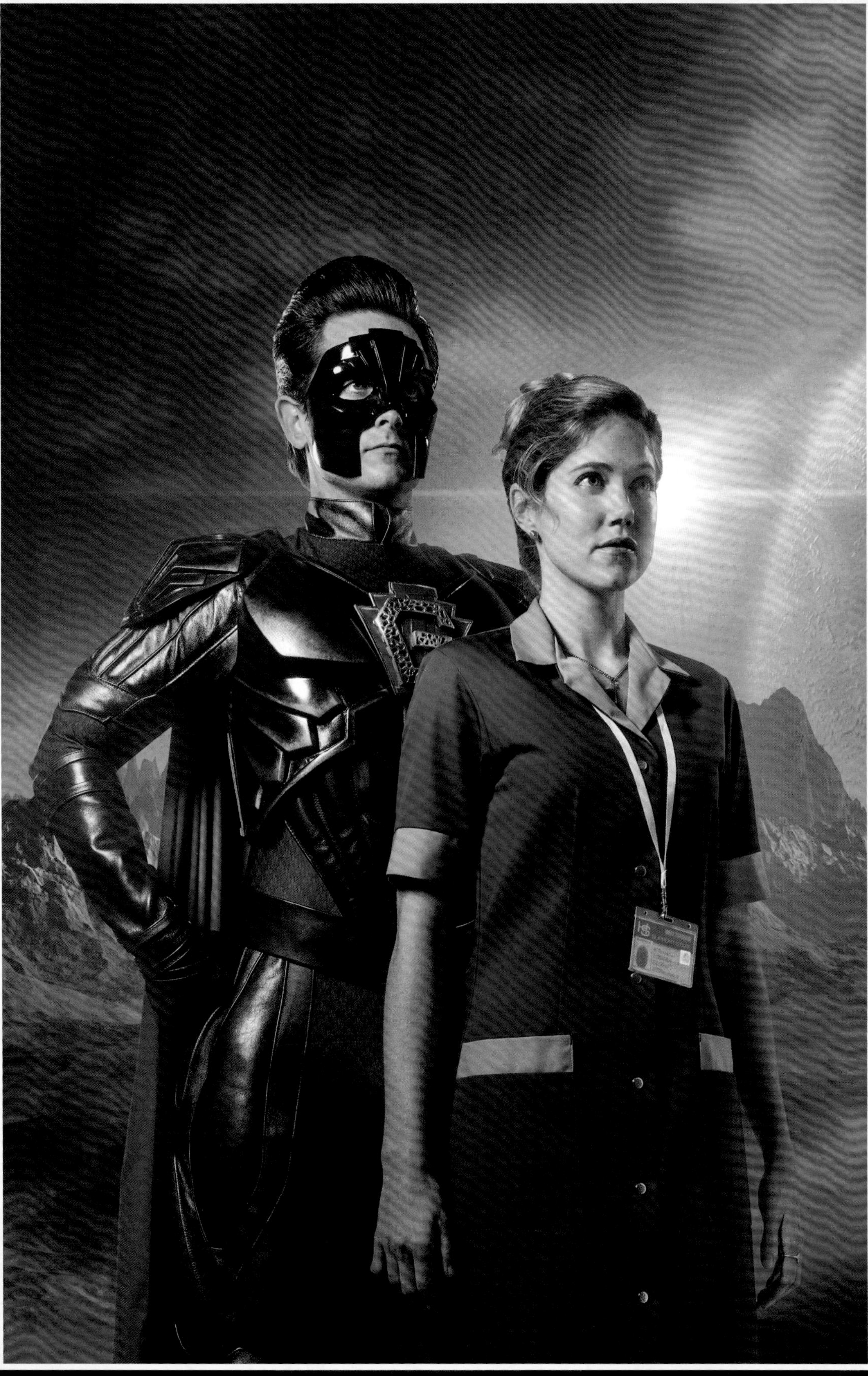

#4 Cover B: AJ

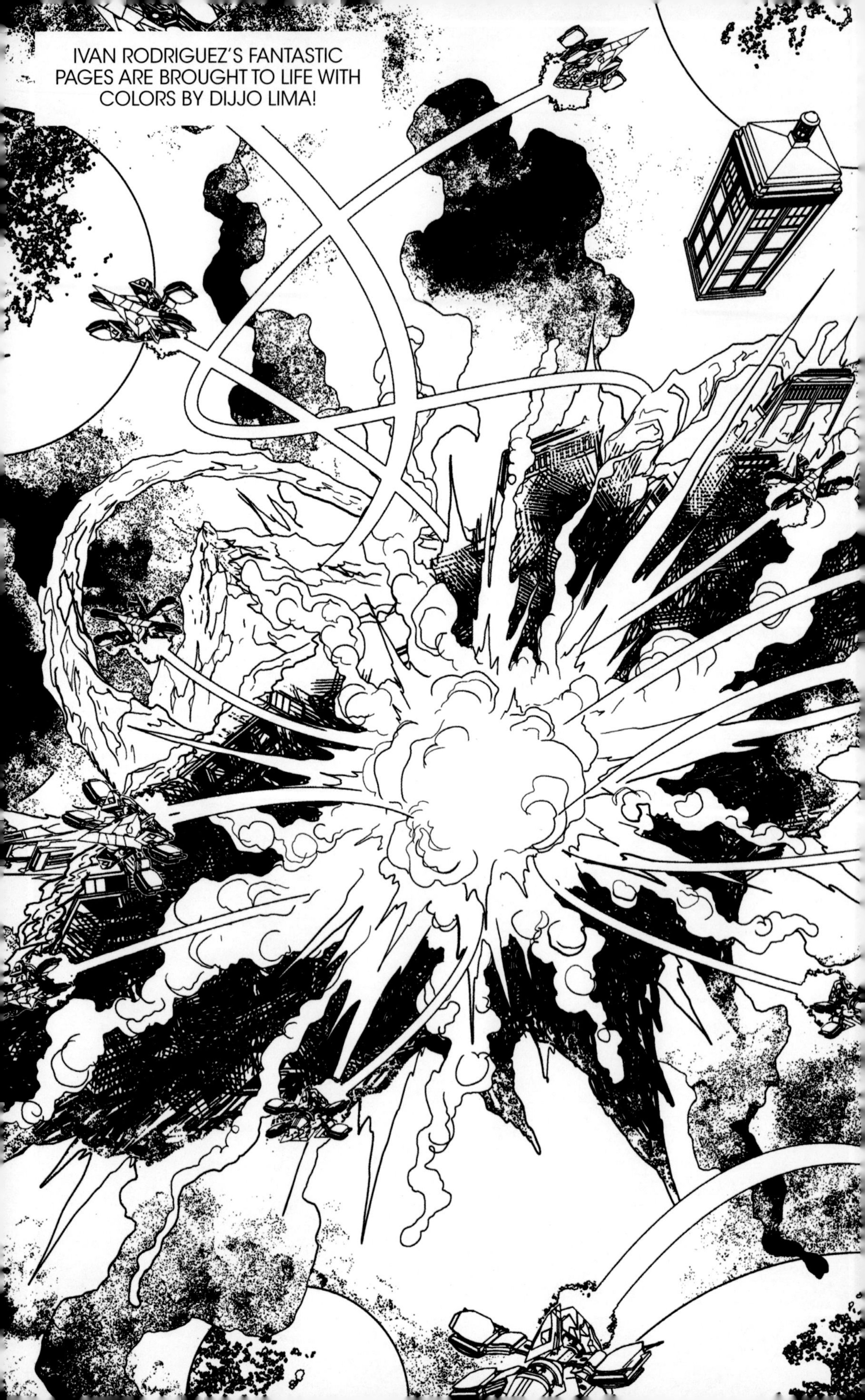
IVAN RODRIGUEZ'S FANTASTIC PAGES ARE BROUGHT TO LIFE WITH COLORS BY DIJJO LIMA!

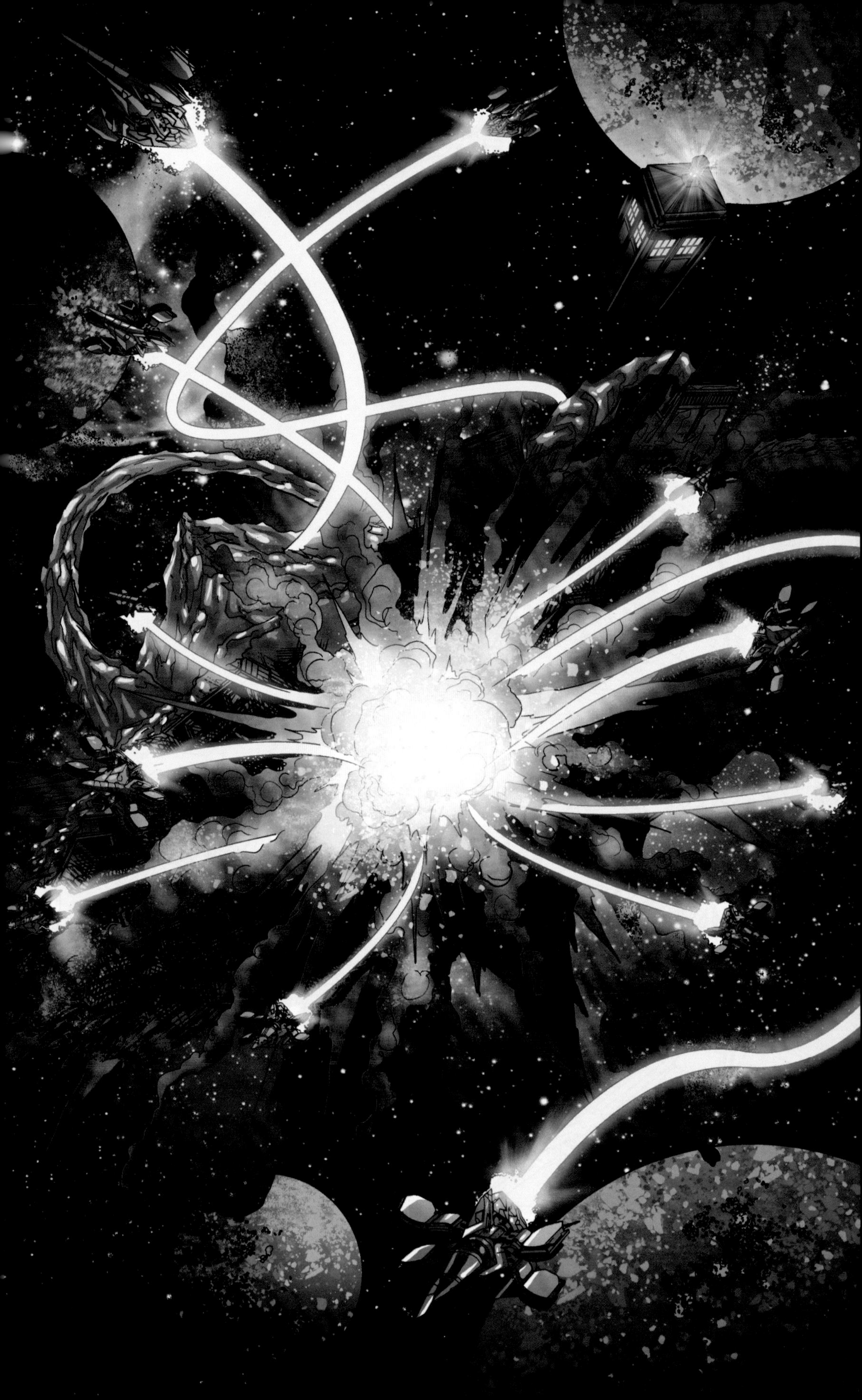

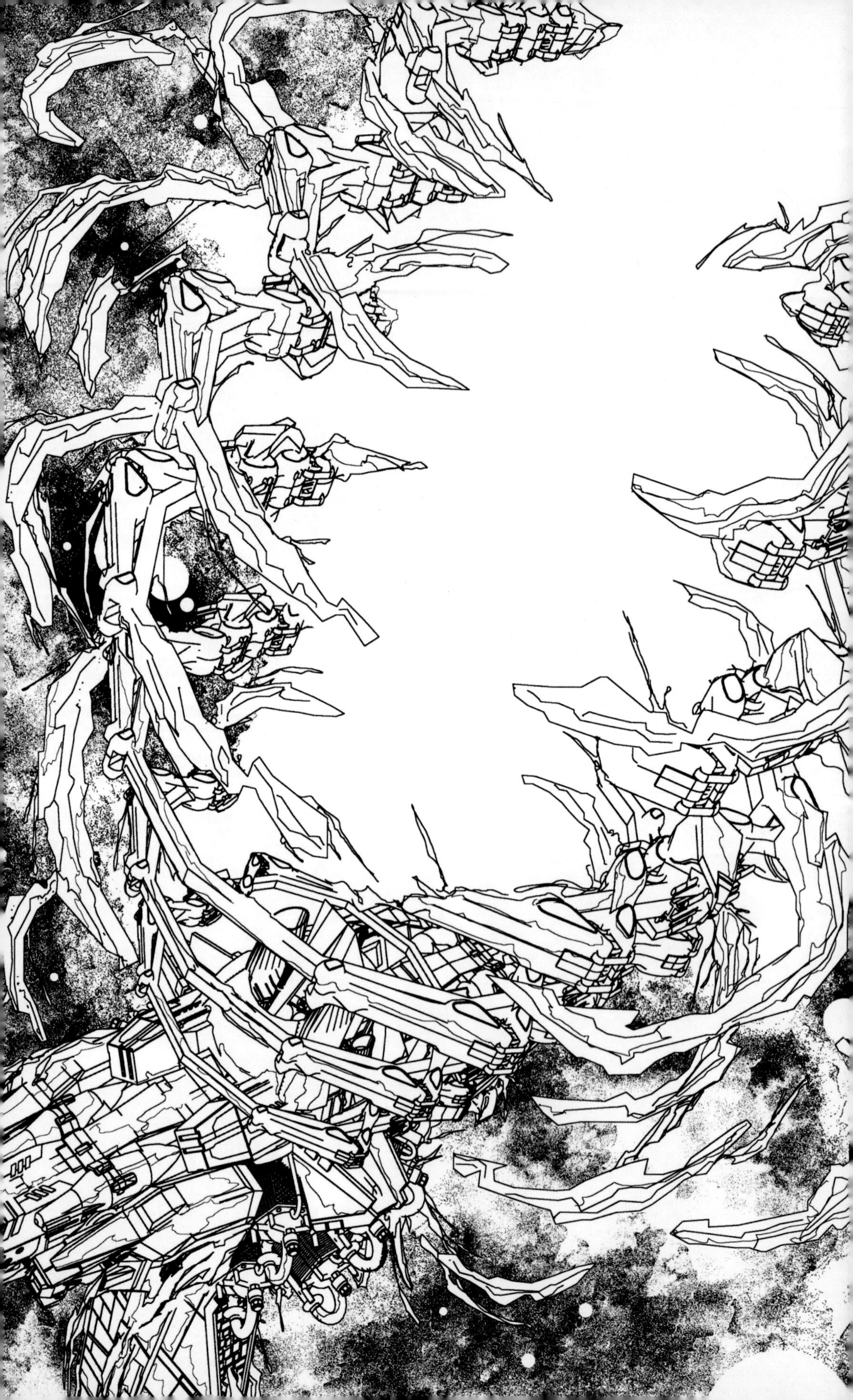

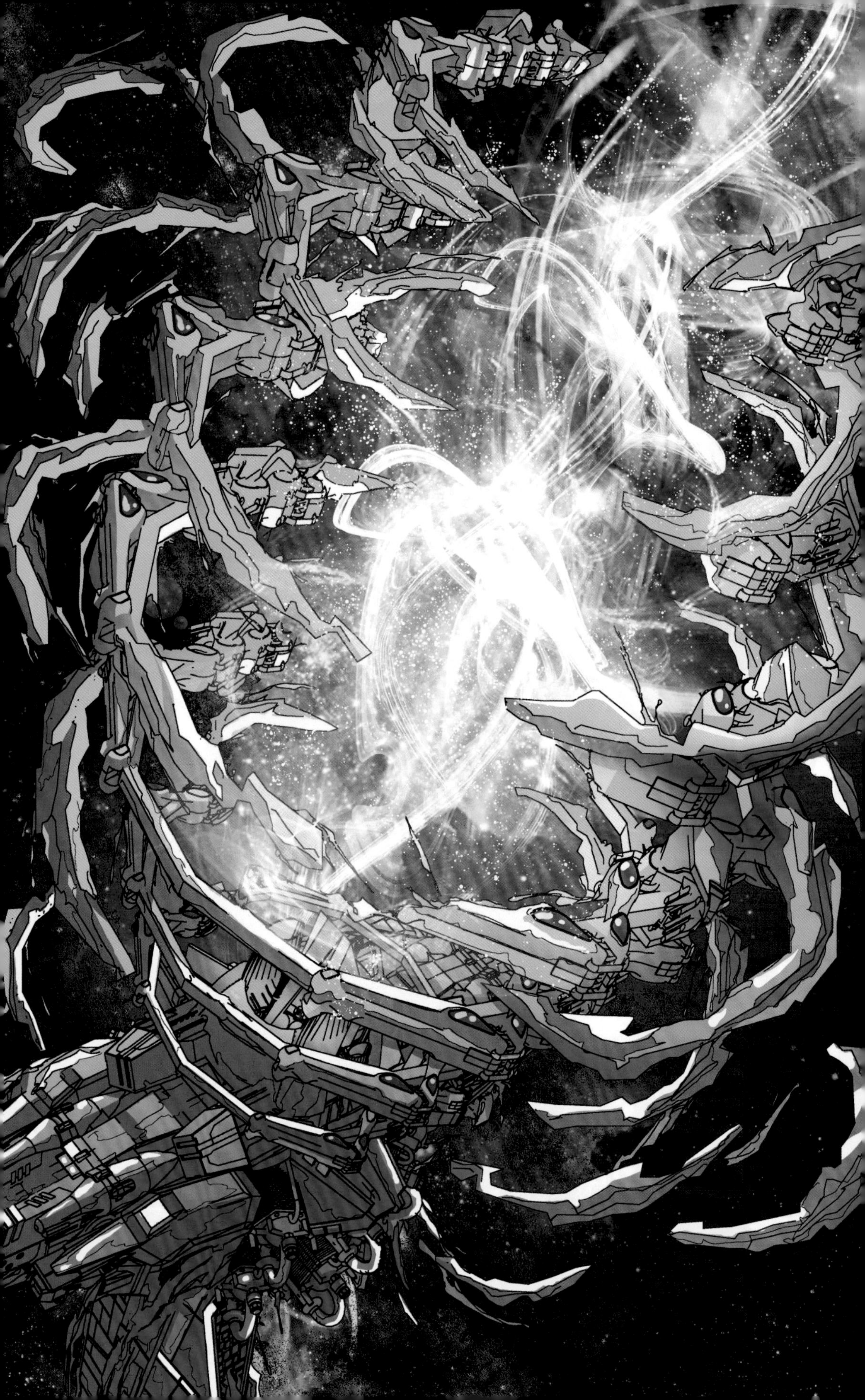

COVER GALLERY

ISSUE #1

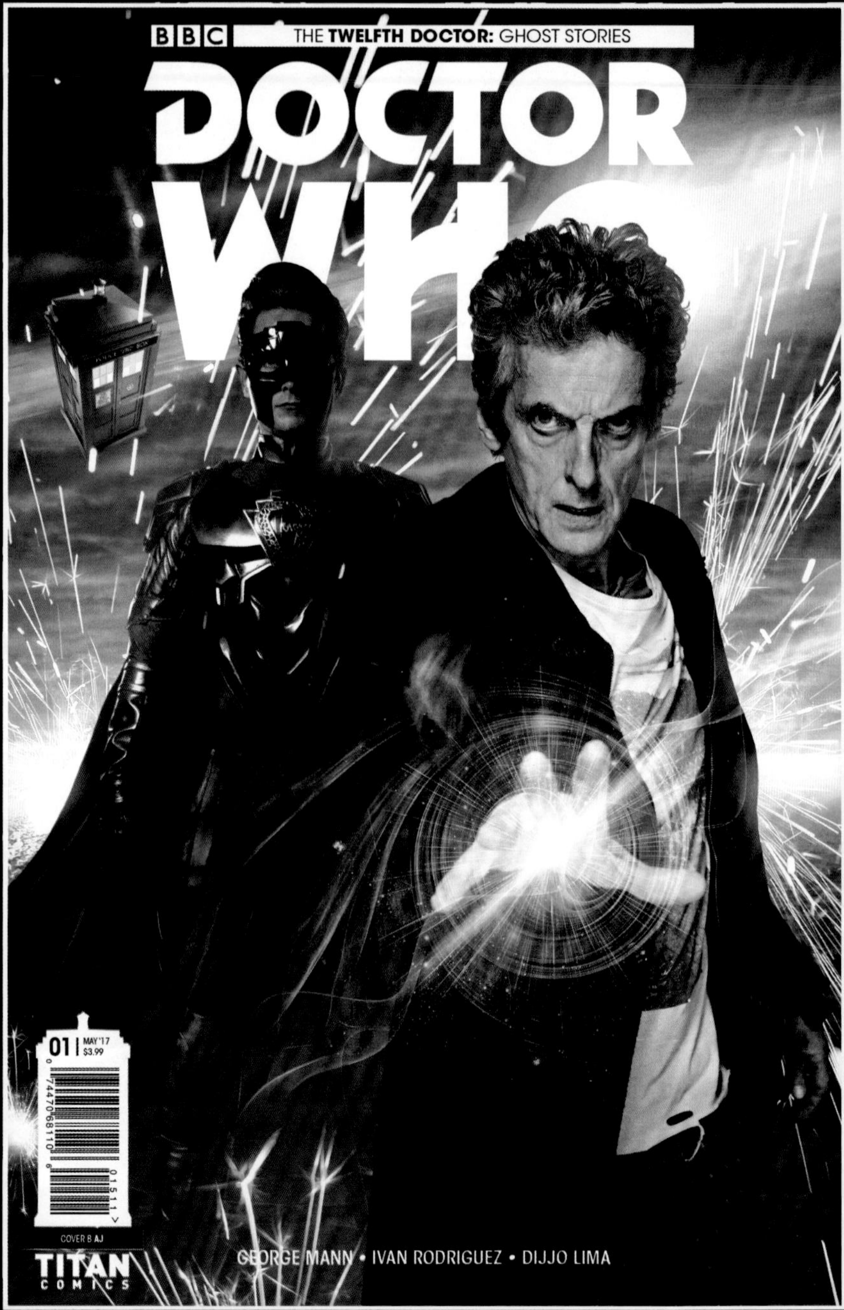
THE TWELFTH DOCTOR: GHOST STORIES
DOCTOR WHO
01 MAY '17 $3.99
COVER B AJ
TITAN COMICS
GEORGE MANN • IVAN RODRIGUEZ • DIJJO LIMA

B. AJ

COVER GALLERY

BBC
THE TWELFTH DOCTOR: GHOST STORIES
DOCTOR WHO
01 MAY'17 $3.99
GEORGE MANN • IVAN RODRIGUEZ • DIJJO LIMA
TITAN COMICS

C. SIMON MYERS

BBC
THE TWELFTH DOCTOR: GHOST STORIES
DOCTOR WHO
LATER ...
HERE I COME!
THE BIG CITY
01 MAY'17 $3.99
GEORGE MANN • IVAN RODRIGUEZ • DIJJO LIMA
TITAN

D. ANTONIO FUSO

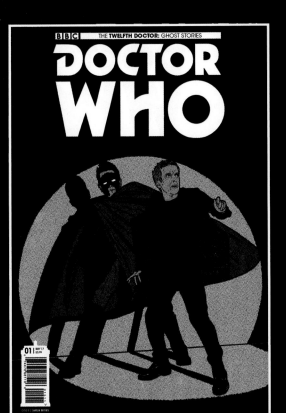

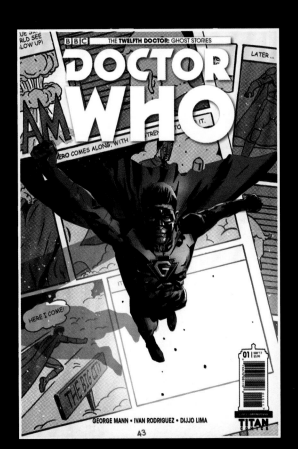

BBC DOCTOR WHO THE TWELFTH DOCTOR

COVER GALLERY

ISSUE #1

BBC
THE TWELFTH DOCTOR: GHOST STORIES
DOCTOR WHO
01 MAY '17 $3.99
TITAN COMICS
GEORGE MANN • IVAN RODRIGUEZ • DIJJO LIMA

E. LUIS GUERRERO

BBC
THE TWELFTH DOCTOR: GHOST STORIES
DOCTOR WHO
PREVIEWS EXCLUSIVE
GEORGE MANN • IVAN RODRIGUEZ • DIJJO LIMA

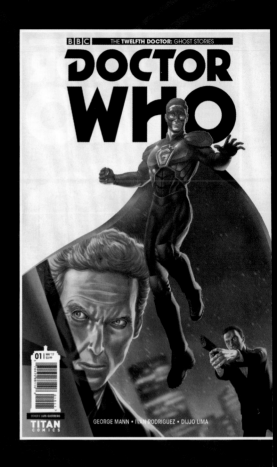

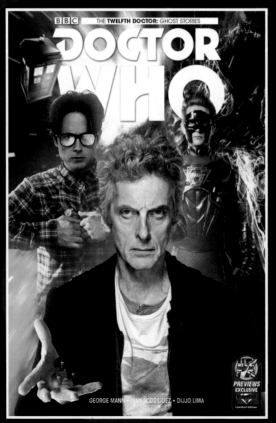

DIAMOND UK EXCLUSIVE PHOTO COVER

COVER GALLERY

ISSUE #2

BBC
THE TWELFTH DOCTOR: GHOST STORIES
DOCTOR WHO
02 | JUN '17 $3.99
COVER C
ANTONIO FUSO
GEORGE MANN • PASQUALE QUALANO • DIJJO LIMA
TITAN COMICS

C. ANTONIO FUSO

BBC
THE TWELFTH DOCTOR: GHOST STORIES
DOCTOR WHO
02 | JUN '17 $3.99
TITAN COMICS
GEORGE MANN • PASQUALE QUALANO • DIJJO LIMA
COVER D
LUIS GUERRERO

D. LUIS GUERRERO

BBC
DOCTOR WHO
THE TWELFTH DOCTOR

COVER GALLERY

ISSUE #3

BBC
THE TWELFTH DOCTOR: GHOST STORIES
DOCTOR WHO
03 JUL '17 $3.99
COVER C
DENNIS CALERO
GEORGE MANN • DENNIS CALERO • DIJJO LIMA
TITAN COMICS

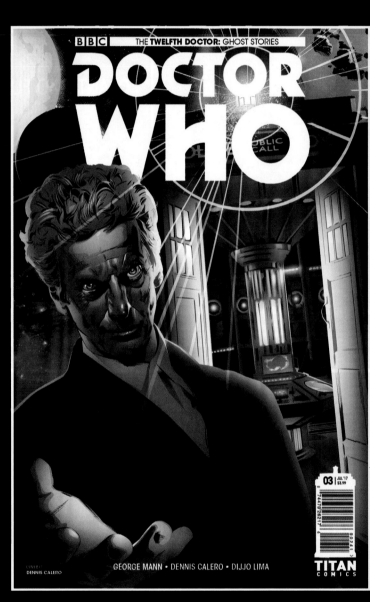

C. DENNIS CALERO

ISSUE #4

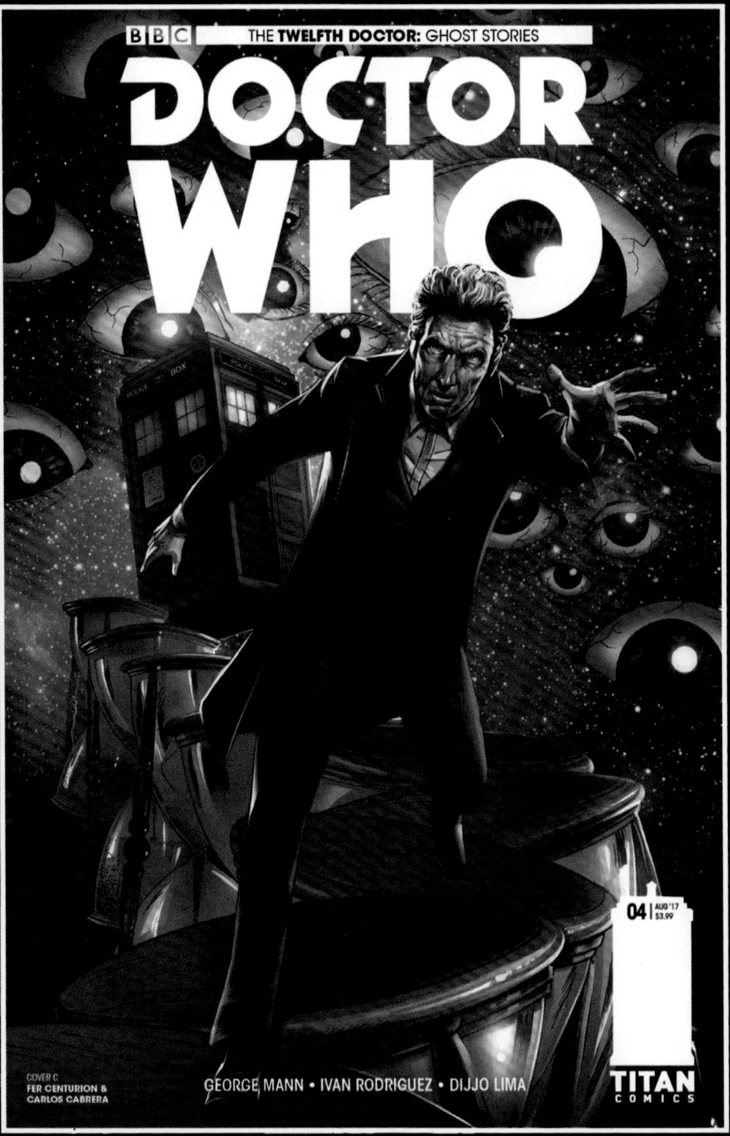
BBC
THE TWELFTH DOCTOR: GHOST STORIES
DOCTOR WHO
04 | AUG '17 $3.99
COVER C
FER CENTURION & CARLOS CABRERA
GEORGE MANN • IVAN RODRIGUEZ • DIJJO LIMA
TITAN COMICS

C. FER CENTURION & CARLOS CABRERA

COVER GALLERY

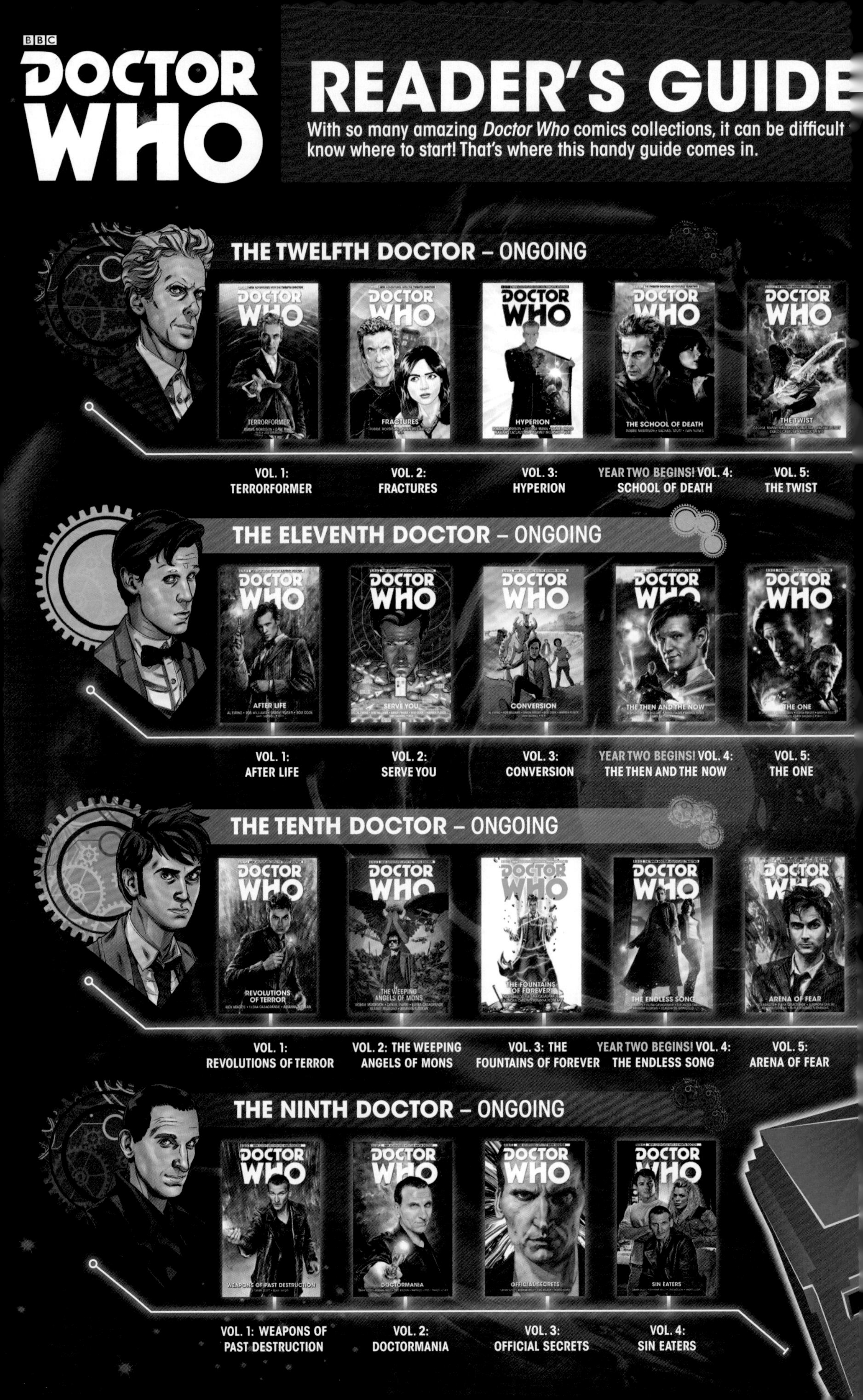

BBC
DOCTOR WHO
READER'S GUIDE
With so many amazing *Doctor Who* comics collections, it can be difficult
know where to start! That's where this handy guide comes in.
THE TWELFTH DOCTOR – ONGOING
VOL. 1: TERRORFORMER
VOL. 2: FRACTURES
VOL. 3: HYPERION
YEAR TWO BEGINS! VOL. 4: SCHOOL OF DEATH
VOL. 5: THE TWIST
THE ELEVENTH DOCTOR – ONGOING
VOL. 1: AFTER LIFE
VOL. 2: SERVE YOU
VOL. 3: CONVERSION
YEAR TWO BEGINS! VOL. 4: THE THEN AND THE NOW
VOL. 5: THE ONE
THE TENTH DOCTOR – ONGOING
VOL. 1: REVOLUTIONS OF TERROR
VOL. 2: THE WEEPING ANGELS OF MONS
VOL. 3: THE FOUNTAINS OF FOREVER
YEAR TWO BEGINS! VOL. 4: THE ENDLESS SONG
VOL. 5: ARENA OF FEAR
THE NINTH DOCTOR – ONGOING
VOL. 1: WEAPONS OF PAST DESTRUCTION
VOL. 2: DOCTORMANIA
VOL. 3: OFFICIAL SECRETS
VOL. 4: SIN EATERS

here are currently **four** ongoing *Doctor Who* series, each following a different Doctor.
ach ongoing series is **entirely self-contained**, so you can follow one, two, or all of your favorite Doctors, as you
ish! The ongoings are arranged in season-like **Years**, collected into roughly three books per Year. Feel free to start at
olume 1 of any series, or jump straight to Volume 4, for an equally-accessible new season premiere!
ach book, and every comic, features a **catch-up and character guide** at the beginning, making it easy to jump
n board – and each ongoing has a very different flavor, representative of that Doctor's era on screen.

VOL. 6:
SONIC BOOM

VOL. 6:
THE MALIGNANT TRUTH

VOL. 6:
SINS OF THE FATHER

THIRD DOCTOR

THE HERALDS OF DESTRUCTION
PAUL CORNELL • CHRISTOPHER JONES • HI-FI

As well as the four ongoing series,
we have published three major
past Doctor miniseries, for the
Third, Fourth, and Eighth Doctors.
These volumes are each a
complete and **self-contained** story.

There are also two fantastic
crossover event volumes, starring
the Ninth, Tenth, Eleventh, and
Twelfth Doctors – the first, *Four
Doctors*, sees an impossible team-
up, and the second, *Supremacy of
the Cybermen*, sees the monstrous
cyborgs rule victorious over the
universe… unless the Doctors
can stop them!

FOURTH DOCTOR

GAZE OF THE MEDUSA
GORDON RENNIE • EMMA BEEBY • BRIAN WILLIAMSON • HI-FI

FOUR DOCTORS

PAUL CORNELL ∎ NEIL EDWARDS
FOUR DOCTORS
WITH IVAN NUNES AND COMICRAFT

EIGHTH DOCTOR

A MATTER OF LIFE AND DEATH
GEORGE MANN • EMMA VIECELI • HI-FI

SUPREMACY OF
THE CYBERMEN

GEORGE MANN ∎ CAVAN SCOTT ∎ IVAN RODRIGUEZ
WALTER GEOVANNI ∎ ALESSANDRO VITTI
SUPREMACY OF THE CYBERMEN
WITH NICOLA RIGHI AND COMICRAFT

VISIT **TITAN-COMIC.COM**

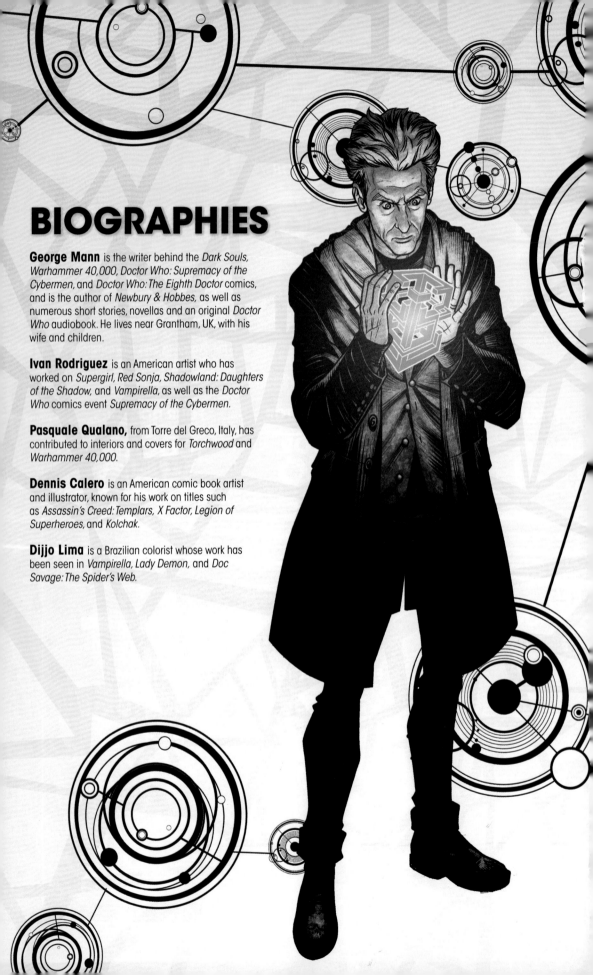

BIOGRAPHIES

George Mann is the writer behind the *Dark Souls*, *Warhammer 40,000*, *Doctor Who: Supremacy of the Cybermen*, and *Doctor Who: The Eighth Doctor* comics, and is the author of *Newbury & Hobbes*, as well as numerous short stories, novellas and an original *Doctor Who* audiobook. He lives near Grantham, UK, with his wife and children.

Ivan Rodriguez is an American artist who has worked on *Supergirl*, *Red Sonja*, *Shadowland: Daughters of the Shadow*, and *Vampirella*, as well as the *Doctor Who* comics event *Supremacy of the Cybermen*.

Pasquale Qualano, from Torre del Greco, Italy, has contributed to interiors and covers for *Torchwood* and *Warhammer 40,000*.

Dennis Calero is an American comic book artist and illustrator, known for his work on titles such as *Assassin's Creed: Templars*, *X Factor*, *Legion of Superheroes*, and *Kolchak*.

Dijjo Lima is a Brazilian colorist whose work has been seen in *Vampirella*, *Lady Demon*, and *Doc Savage: The Spider's Web*.